AF597520

Die Reihe „Kulturwissenschaft interdisziplinär" wird herausgegeben von

The series „Interdisciplinary Studies on Culture and Society"
is edited by

Caroline Y. Robertson-von Trotha

Band 5

Volume 5

Caroline Y. Robertson-von Trotha [ed.]

In collaboration with Christine Mielke

Europe:
Insights from the Outside

Die Deutsche Nationalbibliothek verzeichnet diese Publikation in der Deutschen Nationalbibliografie; detaillierte bibliografische Daten sind im Internet über http://dnb.d-nb.de abrufbar.

Die Deutsche Nationalbibliothek lists this publication in the Deutsche Nationalbibliografie; detailed bibliographic data is available in the Internet at http://dnb.d-nb.de.

ISBN 978-3-8329-5583-0

Übersetzung ins Englische:
Kareem James Abu-Zeid; LINKE & SCHREIER Fachübersetzungen für Kunst, Kultur und Wissenschaften

1. Auflage 2011

Contents

Europe: Insights from the Outside – An Introduction

Caroline Y. Robertson-von Trotha

I.

This volume unites the contributions to the 11th and 12th 'Karlsruhe Dialogues', which took place under the title 'My Europe – Your Europe'. The Karlsruhe Dialogues were initiated in 1997 by the ZAK | Centre for Cultural and General Studies at the Karlsruhe Institute of Technology (KIT) and are organised once a year in cooperation with other cultural institutions in the city of Karlsruhe. Through an open and reflective discourse that has given rise to the contributions in this book – and also by featuring performances from the arts, including film, readings, music, and theatre – the Karlsruhe Dialogues support a creative quest for insights and new approaches aimed at solving controversial issues within society at large. Scholars and experts from communities of practise and from civil society organisations highlight various aspects of the chosen topic, and both complementary and contradictory points of view are presented. In a globalised world, the transdisciplinary perspective of culture has taken on increased significance with regards to the interrelatedness of the local and the global. The recognition of the connections between the local and the global has become central to comparative cultural studies as a whole, as well as to our understanding of the co-evolution of science and society.[1] The inclusion of a sensual access to the topic through the often provocative contributions from the arts, and the opening introduction with an universal interdisciplinary overview make the Karlsruhe Dialogues unique. Their aim: to promote science in dialogue.

The original presentations and the written versions printed here were developed on the basis of a concept that goes beyond a thematically organised panorama of Europe's socio-cultural make-up, particularly in relation to multicultural and transcultural phenomena. The specificity of this concept and of this volume is that only persons with a non-European background were asked to reflect on perceptions, cultural values,[2] expectations, and developments of the European entity. In the first year of the programme, only non-Europeans living outside the continent were invi-

1 See *Helga Nowotny/Peter Scott/Peter Gibbons*: Re-thinking Science. Knowledge and the Public in an Age of Uncertainty, Cambridge 2001. See also *Caroline Y. Robertson-von Trotha*: Schlüsselqualifikationen revisited. Ein altes Thema in Zukunftskontexten, in: *ibid.* (ed.): Schlüsselqualifikationen für Studium, Beruf und Gesellschaft. Technische Universitäten im Kontext der Kompetenzdiskussion (= Problemkreise der Angewandten Kulturwissenschaft 14), Karlsruhe 2009, pp. 17-57.

2 The written contribution by Hans Lenk, former holder of the Chair of Philosophy at the University of Karlsruhe (now the Karlsruhe Institute of Technology) and President of the World Society of Philosophy is the only exception.

ted to speak. Their perspectives as 'outsiders' enabled them to 'open the eyes' of both people of European ethnic origins and those with a migrant background who however were socialised to a lesser or larger extent within Europe, revealing a number of new perceptions. The speakers gave voice to the expectations that a globalised world has of Europe. Additionally, Europeans' myths about themselves were often called into question and amended. This picture was supplemented in the Dialogues of the following year by a focus on immigrants within Europe, i.e. on those whose lives are now centred in a European country.[3]

By bringing together both European migrant perspectives and entirely non-European points of view, this volume casts new light on recent developments within the EU and on decisions the EU is taking about its direction in the coming years and decades, and opens these developments and decisions up to increased scrutiny. These unfamiliar perspectives help expose the limits of myths cherished by individuals or whole societies while at the same time sharpening perceptions of cultural heritage and its loss. Unacceptable cultural practises are also called into question in this way, opening up one of the major and most controversial European debates with regard to integration and its limits.

For all of these reasons, the Karlsruhe Dialogues were able to contribute to the 'European Year of Intercultural Dialogue' in 2008. In addition to this, they were among the cultural 'beacon projects' while Germany held the Presidency of the Council of the European Union in the first half of 2007. The Dialogues also enjoyed the patronage of the German Commission for UNESCO in both 2007 and 2008.

General key questions provided the stimulus for all the authors whose contributions have been published here: What is characteristic of Europe and what positive qualities distinguish it? How do migrants – whether those with or without citizenship in a European country – evaluate and perceive life among their new neighbours? Many associate Europe with the dream of freedom and egalitarianism. For others, Europe is a continent of double standards, where legal freedoms certainly do not apply equally to all groups in everyday life. The general public often prefers to look away when these rights are violated – whether by the host society or by members of the immigrant communities. Does this situation lead to the impression that the presupposed 'European Dream' is nothing but an illusion? And what is understood by the concept of freedom and human rights in different cultural groups? Necla Kelek points out that the concept of freedom is culturally conditioned.[4] It implicitly addresses issues of intellectual and corporal autonomy that arise within

3 *Robertson-von Trotha, Caroline Y.*: Die Dialektik der Globalisierung. Kulturelle Nivellierung bei gleichzeitiger Verstärkung kultureller Differenz, Karlsruhe 2009.

4 See Necla Kelek's text 'The Freedom that I Mean… or *The Heart – or Wurst – of the Matter*' in this volume, pp. 81-92.

the socialisation process. If immigrants have never experienced Western-style independence and self-responsibility themselves, then they often have inherent fears on the individual level, which makes discussion of these issues on the transcultural level very difficult. Thus, the Universal Declaration of Human Rights is often dismissed as a culturally conditioned document of Western societies. This is discussed in the contribution by Hans Lenk, who addresses the question of the common characteristics of Europe's unity of values.

The speakers were also asked whether Europe is a continent in transition, a multicultural construct, or a geopolitical entity with global responsibilities. With reference to the pluricultural experience of India, Anil Bhatti points out that discussing culture and diversity implies a discussion about what he calls the "renegotiation of the coordinates of life world."[5] Hybridity and the complexity of change on the one hand, and cultural stigmatisation and xenophobia that reinforce the reaction of self-chosen isolation on the other hand (an isolation that includes the organisation and strengthening of cultural-ethnic identities), are all part and parcel of the mosaic of European civil societies. They cannot be fully understood without reference to both collective and individual pasts, and to the memories and anxieties these pasts encompass. The life world is a question of perspective. Or, according to the words of Bhatti: a map of the world from the perspective of New Zealand looks very different from a map centred on Europe.[6]

II.

Europe is a complex political, geographical, cultural, and socio-economic entity, to mention only a few of the attributes that could be named. It is a continent that has undergone rapid change in the past decades: due to glasnost and perestroika, technological developments, demographic trends, work migration, and globalisation – again mentioning only some of the major motors of change. It is a continent which has in the past twenty years been particularly concerned with itself and its own far-reaching processes of transformation, centred around the reunification of Germany and the end of bloc politics after the fall of the Berlin Wall. European nation states have experienced change both within their own boundaries and shifts with regard to their levels of sovereignty within the political entity of the European Union. European societies have undergone massive transitions at varying speeds. Simultaneously common values and very differing models of civil society exist among EU member states; coalitions of alignment vary over time; and there are many disparate, and often radically differing, images of the continent's future development. Europe increasingly has to address questions both with regard to integration within the process of European unification and with regard to its role in a globalised world society. By focusing on its commitment to the concept of 'diversity in unity' on the

5 See Anil Bhatti's text 'Remarks on Culture and Diversity' in this volume, pp. 43-50, p. 43.
6 Ibid.

basis of the Universal Declaration of Human Rights, critics have called into question many of Europe's self-perceptions and collective memories, as well as many of its practical actions at home and abroad.

The geopolitical and socio-cultural nature of Europe cannot be analysed and critically questioned without close attention to its medial dimension. Images are ubiquitous in our globalised, media-driven information society. The internet and in particular the exponential growth of new social networks have led to a massive increase both in the availability and distribution of information. These trends have also led to a resurgence in what could be called organised propaganda, with new forms of politicisation and emotional mobilisation becoming visible. Some refer to an extension of the Cold War, or to the 'clash of civilisations' now being fought with new means. Irresponsible and responsible reporting in the traditional media can excite latent emotions very quickly and unexpectedly – the deep impression of the images of September 11th is a case in point. Developments in communications are also making it increasingly difficult to separate domestic and foreign policy in terms of their consequences. Satellite technologies allow whole immigrant communities to follow events 'at home' in their mother tongues as if they had never migrated. The consequences for processes of adaptation to a new local cultural environment are far-reaching: the impetus to learn the language of the host country and take an interest in its everyday affairs is greatly reduced. Furthermore, this often affects the following generation by strengthening the tendency to form ethnic colonies. Local events are unexpectedly interpreted in larger geopolitical contexts that are either unforeseeable or whose significance, with reference to cultural identities, is often underestimated. This is no less true of genuinely unacceptable situations that have established themselves and become structurally significant over the course of time than it is for the misuse of local events for purposes of a tendentious politicisation. Our memories of past events, positive or negative, make up our identities. The primarily subjective preconceptions that develop in this way are essential ingredients in our sense of community, in our perception, and in our actions as human beings.

Living together in local communities has become more complex in Europe. Europe is rich and diverse in terms of ethnicity and culture. This shared public space has become less and less forgiving of omissions and misjudgements in integration policy. In nearly all European countries, integration is now understood as one of the key tasks of our time. In Germany, the first ever national integration plan has now been developed. It was devised in cooperation with immigrants and immigrant organisations and was presented to the public in July 2007.[7] The "necessity of a col-

7 7. Bericht der Beauftragten der Bundesregierung für Migration, Flüchtlinge und Integration über die Lage der Ausländerinnen und Ausländer in Deutschland, December 2007, pp. 35; http://www.bundesregierung.de/Content/DE/Publikation/IB/Anlagen/auslaenderbericht-7,property=publicationFile.pdf [15. 10. 2010].

lective and coherent approach to integration policy as well as the continuing importance of shared fundamental principles as the basis for the European integration effort"[8] has been emphasised at the international and European levels. Within the EU, national strategies for integration policy differ sharply from one nation to another, and range from the strongly assimilationist approaches of countries such as France to the much less assimilationist policies of the United Kingdom and others. The British model of a society based on the principle of multiculturalism has faced criticism since the bombing attacks on the London Underground in 2005 and the attack on Glasgow Airport in 2007. Both of these attacks were carried out by so-called 'home-grown terrorists' – young British citizens from immigrant families – and the perpetrators could not in any way be described as young adults with no prospects for the future, an observation that also pertains to those who carried out the September 11th attacks.[9]

The implementation of integration policies reveals serious deficits in all EU countries, although these efforts have been given high priority in some places. In this context, the development of a coherent strategy at the level of EU policy is an urgent and formidable task. Several issues need to be clarified: How should we define integration? Which cultural differences ought to be protected in keeping with UNESCO principles, for example, and which differences are incompatible with pluralistic constitutional democracy? How can we learn from the experiences of other countries? The aim of setting up contemporary standards of informed cultural best practices is paramount for transcultural understanding. And how can we establish an on-going dialogue on the subject? This dialogue should include insights from outside of Europe that give impetus to rational political counsel at both the international and local levels.[10] Furthermore, and most challenging of all, how do we involve citizens from all cultural backgrounds? None of these questions are new.

---

8 Ibid., p. 284. The German original reads: "Notwendigkeit eines globalen und kohärenten Ansatzes in der Integrationspolitik und die weiterhin bestehende Wichtigkeit der gemeinsamen Grundprinzipien als Grundlage für den europäischen Integrationsansatz".

9 In these cases young intellectuals either as students or already established within a profession were involved.

10 A European example at the local level is CLIP (Cities for Local Integration Policy), a network of 30 European cities working together to support the social and economic integration of migrants; http://www.eurofound.europa.eu/areas/populationandsociety/clip.htm [15. 10. 2010]. Of particular importance is the UNESCO Convention leading in Germany to the White Paper 'Shaping Cultural Diversity' which was co-authored by scholars and practitioners from many areas and makes concrete recommendations for action: *German Commission for UNESCO* (ed.): Shaping Cultural Diversity. Recommendations for Action from Civil Society for the Implementation in and by Germany of the UNESCO Convention on the Diversity of Cultural Expressions (2005), White Paper, Bonn 2010; http://www.unesco.de/fileadmin/medien/Dokumente/Bibliothek/unesco_weissbuch_Englisch_2010.pdf [15. 10. 2010]. The Anna Lindh Foundation (ALF) is a younger and ambitious institutional network intending "to bring people together from across the Mediterranean to improve mutual respect between cultures and to support civil society working for a common future of the region." See also the Anna Lindh Report 2010 'Euromed Intercultural Trends'; http://www.euromedalex.org/sites/default/files/AnnaLindhReport2010.pdf [15. 10. 2010].

The issue of cultural diversity and integration includes a deeply political dimension alongside its more moral and practical aspects. In February 2008, the Turkish Prime Minister, Recep Tayyip Erdogan, illustrated this fact with his declaration that "assimilation is a crime against humanity" in front of approximately 20,000 Turks gathered to see him in Cologne, Germany. And in Holland, the murder of the Dutch filmmaker Theo van Gogh just two years after the assassination of the right-wing politician Pim Fortyn emotionalised the cultural pluralism debate and led to broader levels of solidarity against liberal cultural policy.

With the publication of Thilo Sarrazin's book *Deutschland schafft sich ab* in August 2010, an unusually broad and highly controversial debate on integration has been ignited in Germany, a debate that involves all political parties. This includes the German Social Democratic Party (*Sozialdemokratische Partei Deutschlands*, SPD), which wants to expel Sarrazin from the party. More interesting is the fact that Sarrazin's assumption that many Arab and Turkish immigrants are unwilling to integrate, is prevalent among many Germans, most of whom have not read Sarrazin's book (and are therefore not necessarily supporting his hypotheses on the hereditary role of genes in the distribution of intelligence). These examples, which could be supplemented by many more, underline one of the few general theorems accepted by almost all sociologists: cultural, ethnic, and national identities are open to politicisation and mobilisation.

A number of basic and conflicting issues can be outlined concisely: The first of the dilemmas facing Europe with regard to integration can be effectively illustrated through the biographies of many of the contributing authors. Several of them have chosen to live in Europe because they face restrictions or even severe persecution in their native countries. Others have grown up in Europe, but find themselves subject to death threats because traditionally oriented families and in particular fundamentalist groups within the immigrant communities have imported practises in violation of basic human rights to Europe, and unquestioningly defend these practises as a part of their culture: now, in many communities of third generation immigrants, the conflict between modernising reformists and orthodox traditionalists has become more acute and not less. Women feel threatened because they are no longer prepared to remain silent in the face of the unjust traditional practices of patriarchally structured immigrant communities. Migrants themselves are often out of touch with the extent of the changes and varying perceptions that are being articulated in their countries of origin. The balance among orthodox traditionalists, fundamentalists, and modernising reformists is changing as part of a complex non-linear process of self-segregation and desegregation, of construction and deconstruction. Within migrant communities, very different and often controversial views of the role of culture and questions of integration prevail. These are deeply influenced both by local conditions in the chosen countries of migration and the initial impetus for migration. They include more general complex underlying attitudes toward the balance between protecting one's own cultural heritage and being open to the dynamics of change, a dialectical process that involves local communities, national state policies, and framework conditions. The issue of integration taken as a complex whole has many facets and cannot be effectively considered on the basis of generalisations. Shared everyday cultural values and principles make up an important part of this whole.

The second dilemma surrounding the issue of integration is the fact that structures of segregation contributing to the development of 'parallel societies' can be identified and that there have been active efforts to further develop these segregational tendencies among some groups.[11] There is a growing awareness that the various failures of states and mainstream European cultures to recognise and embrace contemporary cultural diversity as part of a historical process initially contributed to this development, but this does not change the current situation. The formulation of appropriate measures of inclusive social and cultural policies are needed. A discussion on the implementation of incentives and also strict sanctions is part of this debate. Moreover, in political practise, diversity has yet to be recognised for its value and potential; it is merely portrayed as a manifest challenge to the fabric of society. In this respect it must be remembered that many European countries, especially those of Eastern Europe, still regard themselves as culturally homogeneous – and this claim can indeed be substantiated to some extent by migration statistics.

The third dilemma surrounding the issue of integration is the progressive strengthening of stereotypes and prejudices on both sides. This development calls for determined efforts to discredit and debunk such stereotypes, which play a central role in the unequal opportunities characteristic not only of the educational system and the job market, but also of the housing market. The thesis of structural discrimination cannot be overlooked, and must be discussed.

With its programmatic decisions regarding the 'European Year of Equal Opportunities for All' in 2007, the European Union initiated increased discussion of proactive measures – these decisions were quite controversial, and need to be discussed in a correspondingly complex manner.[12] Universal equal opportunity encompasses many disparate issues. Gender equality and freedom in the choice of one's partner, for example, remain major challenges for the acceptance of significantly non-integrated communities. For this reason, strategies for the improvement of socio-economic participation need to be discussed alongside strategies addressing the simultaneous problem of socio-cultural barriers. Above all, we need to become more proactive.

---

11 *Bundesministerium des Innern/Bundesministerium der Justiz* (eds.): Zweiter Periodischer Sicherheitsbericht. Kurzfassung, Nov. 2006; http://www.bmj.bund.de/files/-/1481/PSB.pdf [15. 10. 2010].

12 *European Commission* (ed.): Putting Equality into Practice: What Role for Positive Action?, Directorate-General for Employment, Social Affairs and Equal Opportunities, Unit G.4 March 2007; http://biblio.ugent.be/input/download?func=downloadFile&fileOId=733550 [15. 10. 2010].

A particularly disturbing development can be observed in many European societies: racism and the politically motivated criminality of the radical right are on the rise. We are presently experiencing higher levels of cultural discrimination due to the projection of stereotypes and the lack of opportunities to correct these stereotypes. The concentration of ethnic communities in certain – usually socially and economically less attractive – areas with cheaper living accommodation in many European cities reinforces this development.[13] This is equally true of criminal acts motivated by xenophobia and anti-Semitism. Europeans, in particular those with darker complexions, experience discrimination in their everyday lives and are increasingly subject to racist attacks as well. These developments stem from a latent ideology of 'white power' and from a lack of awareness of the historical fact of Europe's ethnic diversity. At the same time, a process that can be described as the dialectics of racism can be increasingly observed.[14] It is not only people from Middle Eastern countries who face discrimination on the basis of their distinctive ethnic appearances, but also those who only vaguely differ from preconceived cultural norms. An increasing Islamophobia can be demonstrated in all European countries. The acclaimed and respected Egyptian academic Nasr H. Abu Zaid, who sadly died this year, points out the paradoxical function that this kind of prejudice and marginalisation appears to be filling: "Europe seems to be well identified only in comparison with Muslims and in the face of Islam; but how much of Europe's identity is actually a reaction against its own history and some of its own citizens?"[15] The problematic nature of orientalism – as something that emerges from the transfiguration of a seemingly oriental (fairy-tale) world and a simultaneous Islamophobia – needs further consideration: the contrast between Europe and the Islamic world cannot be described as a stagnant opposition when the borders between the two are slowly disappearing. The force of potential politicisation remains however, even when cultural difference is diminished.

The French philosopher Bernhard-Henri Lévy, who was born in Algeria, stated the following in an interview on the subject of feelings of belonging: "Tolerance is the weakest form of love"[16] – we are not *tolerant* toward our friends. The motto of 'tough love', for example vocal criticism, the definition of limits, and constructive confrontation, is considered – or at least was considered, prior to the era of political

13 See also the Sinus Sociovision survey 'Die Milieus der Menschen mit Migrationshintergrund in Deutschland'; http://www.bmfsfj.de/bmfsfj/generator/RedaktionBMFSFJ/Abteilung4/Pdf-Anlagen/migranten-milieu-report-2007-pdf,property=pdf,rwb=true.pdf [15. 10. 2010].

14 See for example Nasr H. Abu Zaid's text 'Islam in Europe/Europe Against Islam! Europe, Open Your Eyes' in this volume, pp. 67-73, p. 70: "If things continue to go as badly as they are at the moment, this alienation, and the way it both feeds and is fed by the resentment of mainly white, Christian or post-Christian Europeans, could tear apart the civic fabric of Europe's most established democracies."

15 Ibid., p. 71.

16 *Institut für Auslandsbeziehungen* (ed.): Kulturaustausch. Zeitschrift für internationale Perspektiven, No. 3, Vol. 57, 2007, p. 20.

correctness – a demonstration of respect and affection in the Anglo-Saxon world. This is precisely the type of respect that is directly or indirectly demanded by the contributions in this volume and that could represent – in the form of 'constructive intolerance' – a new, challenging tone of interaction among members of pluralistic societies.

III.

Neither the 11th and 12th Karlsruhe Dialogues nor this publication could have been realised without the commitment and support of the following people and institutions.

I would like to thank the Center for Art and Media Karlsruhe (ZKM | Zentrum für Kunst und Medientechnologie), specifically Peter Weibel and Christiane Riedel. I would also like to thank Thomas Schmid from ARTE Deutschland for his role in the first film evening of the Karlsruhe Dialogues.

I would particularly like to emphasise the contribution of our main sponsor, Sparda Bank: for the fourth time, I have the pleasure of thanking them for being our most generous sponsor. Special thanks go to Thomas Renner. My thanks also go to the city of Karlsruhe. The city has supported and sponsored not only the Karlsruhe Dialogues but also many other activities of our Centre for Cultural and General Studies for several years. The Karlsruhe Dialogues would not be possible without the support of our sponsors, and we thank all of them for the confidence and trust invested in us.

Furthermore, I would like to express my gratitude to the German Commission for UNESCO – and particularly Prof. Dr. Hartwig Lüdtke – for its patronage of the event. Thanks also go to the Anna Lindh Euro-Mediterranean Foundation for the Dialogue Between Cultures.

I would like to thank Kareem James Abu-Zeid for his scrupulous proof-reading of most of the English contributions as well as the English translations of all German texts. Finally, I would like to thank the team of editors of the ZAK – Christine Mielke, Janina Hecht, Sonja Seidel, and Christine Wölfle – for the realisation of this publication and the complex organisational work that it involved.

Karlsruhe, September 2010

Caroline Y. Robertson-von Trotha

Europe/The Outside/Enlightenment[1]

Susan Neiman

A little while ago I visited a conference of German and English opinion makers, people who have been meeting for years in order to promote both German-English relations and also the cause of Europe in general. The role appointed to me was clear: As someone who had spent more of her adult life in Berlin than anywhere else, I was to account for the outsider perspective. I did this gladly, for at the time it seemed to me that my thoughts on the topic urgently needed to be expressed. A new English film about Guantanamo – a film that really got under one's skin – had just started playing, and I was worried. If Danish cartoons had led to rioting and deaths at anti-Western demonstrations across the Islamic world, then what would be triggered by the sight of innocent men being tortured by Americans in a lawless area? To the humiliation of all decent Americans, Guantanamo and Abu Ghraib had become the public face of America, and all the protests and resolutions of the American Congress did little to change this. That was bad enough. But should Guantanamo, Abu Ghraib, and the War in Iraq also have become the public face of the West in general? My view was that Europe must by all means take a stand and clarify that the United States had, for the duration of the Bush administration, lost its right to speak in the name of Western values. Europe may have learned a few lessons in democracy from its American cousins, yet it was now capable of standing on its own two feet, and I believed that it should do this right away by distancing itself from the present American regime – and with more than just a few polite gestures, gestures that deceived no-one. This had absolutely nothing to do with anti-Americanism, but rather with defending those enlightened values that represent the best inheritance of Europe and America. As long as Europe remained spine-less, the West would continue to be measured by the same yardstick as the Bush administration.

I said all this as diplomatically as possible, without the sharpness that the topic deserves, in order to be somewhat conciliatory. The conference was a very courteous event, and my words were courteously ignored, until an English Lord, a member of the upper house of Parliament, took me aside: "I understand quite well what you are trying to say, but it's in vain. England and Germany will never take a real stand together against the Iraq War. We feel too guilty." Guilty? "I understand why the Germans feel guilty," I replied, "although I believe that they are mistaken on this point. But why should the British feel guilty?" "Colonialism," this aristocrat said. "After all, we were the ones who wrongly drew up all of those borders, and we therefore carry a considerable part of the blame for the collapse of the Middle

1 Translated from the German by Kareem James Abu-Zeid.

East. This and the fact that America saved us in World War Two – every one of us would feel guilty if we formed an alliance against America." I took great pains to explain to him that there were many Americans – at the time they were the majority – who would not view such an alliance as an attack on them. On the contrary: Most of them had the impression that their country had been taken in by the government in a way that went against their interests and their values. They would welcome with open arms friendly allies who would stand together with them and bring all of us to our senses in the name of our shared values. Yet my words had no effect. Guilt is a mighty obstacle to this type of negotiation.

America is now looking for new leadership. Yet Europe has apparently decided to keep silent and wait to see if the international political situation improves on its own. The problems of health reform, tax reform, the question of Turkey, the subsequent question of EU expansion, and who knows what else are keeping the politicians in suspense. Yet I ask myself if my English interlocutor had not diagnosed the deeper cause of Europe's silence. The French could have feelings of guilt about Algeria. The Spanish conquest of the New World was one of the most brutal conquests ever. Even the friendly Dutch committed crimes in Indonesia, and tiny Belgium succeeded in turning the Congo into its own personal hell. The Poles view themselves as victims of history and do not seem to feel very guilty about anything, but with time and a bit of effort they too could join the club.

Don't misunderstand me: Self-critique is one of the greatest virtues of the Enlightenment, and nowhere can it be found in a more exemplary fashion than in Europe. The soul-searching that the continent has seen in the last 50 years is indeed one of its greatest achievements – albeit one that is not given much attention at official ceremonies, and for good reason. A nation – or its representatives – would seem intolerably self-righteous and self-satisfied if it congratulated itself on its own self-critique. So allow an outsider to say: With the exception of a few lapses and small differences in tempo, you've done good work.

This is presumably an unprecedented phenomenon, one that would be difficult to conceive of on another continent. (The Japanese are still haggling over what they owe to the women who they forced into prostitution. Try to imagine them conducting their investigations and making amends for these and worse crimes, and then imagine the Chinese reappraising the Cultural Revolution, and Cambodia the Pol Pot Regime, and Myanmar... Only by imagining this happening elsewhere does it dawn on one how much Europe has achieved).

So hats off to you, Europe, for the painful process of self-examination, one that still has a long way to go in some parts of the world. (I would here single out both ends of the continent – Spain and Poland – as countries that still need practice in historical self-critique, although Austria too has yet to do its part.) This is a remarkable phenomenon, and admittedly one with not entirely healthy side effects. As my conversation with the English Lord shows, self-critique can lead to paralysing feelings of guilt. According to my own experience, Europeans are so plagued by self-doubts that they run the risk of becoming idle, not only with regards to foreign affairs in general, but also with regards to many much more fundamental problems. Indeed, most Europeans doubt that there really is a Europe other than an – extremely undefined – geographic unity and a series of economic agreements.

Here too, an outsider perspective can be helpful. Ask an African, an Asian, or an American if Europe exists and you will hear peals of laughter. They will be quick to ignore their own regional differences. What exactly do Louisiana and New York have in common other than – perhaps – language? In matters of history, geography, climate, and culture, Hawaii and Kansas could not be any more different from one another, yet these differences are thought of – if they are thought of at all – in order to praise America's diversity, and not to ask whether the Union should be dissolved.

Humanity's tendency to take its own accomplishments for granted knows few limits. It is thus worthwhile to remember what Europe has to offer: Not only does it have its own cultures, but those of other parts of the world are also remarkably present. No matter how many past sins lie in the word 'Eurocentric', Europe today offers more opportunities to learn from and about other cultures than any other place in the world. On a random evening in Berlin or Paris, films from Mongolia or Senegal can be seen; Iranian poetry or Korean ballet can be enjoyed; and presentations about Croatian literature or labour relations in the U.S. can be heard. All of this adds up to a consciousness of the world that is hard to find anywhere else.

But let us leave our ruminations on political culture aside for a moment and take a look at everyday life. When seen from abroad, any one of the hundred aspects of a European city's everyday life seems to be idyllic. The welfare state is a matter of course for Europeans, yet this has so little to do with the life of an average American – to say nothing at all about that of an Ethiopian or a Bolivian – that most outsiders consider it to be purely utopian. Although Europeans are generally much better informed about the situation in America than Americans are about the situation in Europe, Europeans find the conditions in America so backwards that they can barely understand them. Once, when I wrote an article for a Berlin newspaper about political culture on both sides of the Atlantic, I mentioned an American acquaintance of mine who was grateful to her boss for allowing her to only work half-days for the first six weeks after the birth of her third child. The editor was convinced that this was a typo, and she replaced "six weeks" with "six months". After I had assured her that "six weeks" was exactly what I wanted to write, she got rid of the entire anecdote: European readers would not believe the example and would simply not understand the sentence.

Anyone who has spent enough time with open eyes on both continents can produce any number of similar examples. Even conservative governments would not dare to encroach on the basic social democratic conditions, which are seen as rights and not benefits in the domains of housing, health care, and education. For them, it is not only about defending the principle of equality, but to a much greater extent about defending democracy itself. Any person who needs more than one job to provide for his or her family, or who considers two weeks of vacation a welcome privilege after years of loyal service, presumably does not have much energy to reflect on the political conditions of his or her life. By supporting culture and the freedom necessary to enjoy it, European governments encourage not only recreation and leisure – both of which are worthy of encouragement for their own sakes – but also the fundaments of civic participation. When compared with conditions like these, monstrosities such as malnutrition and homelessness, children who have weapons but no health care, rising population in the prisons, and sinking standards of living make large parts of America look like Hobbes' state of nature.

In this situation, it is possible to see an ironic confirmation of a thesis put forth by Robert Kagan, a neoconservative mouthpiece of the Bush government who caused quite an uproar a few years ago with a book in which he asserted that Americans are Hobbesians and Europeans Kantians. The uninterrupted cycle of fear and subjugation that, according to Hobbes, rules the world does indeed get to the heart of the foreign policy promoted by neoconservatives, whose endless and unpredictable war against terror has a good chance of making life in the foreseeable future "nasty, brutish, and short". For historical reasons, Kagan's transatlantic analyses were met with criticism. Joschka Fischer commented that today's Europeans are everything but descendants of Venus, but are rather much closer to children of Mars: It is not illusions of affluence but rather the memories of two World Wars that form the background of Europe's insistence on peaceful solutions. Yet in spite of its many errors, Kagan's thesis is maintained – and not merely as an object of discussion – in foreign affairs circles across the world, and within the Pentagon as the foundation for some of its political principles.

The way that Kagan's analysis turns history head over heels is more interesting than the individual errors therein. From its beginnings, the United States has been viewed as the embodiment of Enlightenment. Europe may have invented the Enlightenment, but only America was in a position to make it a reality. European thinkers speculated about whether all men were created equal; American thinkers wrote this into law. The American settlers broke with their monarch thirteen years before their French colleagues did the same, just as the Bill of Rights that was composed in Philadelphia inspired the Declaration of the Rights of Man in Paris.

We appear to have a paradox here. On both sides of the Atlantic, the real order of things seems to have been turned upside down. The shedding of blood among neighbours that once defined Europe's foreign policy has given way to various agreements; the injustices and hierarchies that once formed the basis of domestic policy have been replaced by unprecedented social democratic structures. Europe's basic conditions are as Kantian as can be, while America seems to be intent on developing a world that is becoming more and more similar to the Hobbesian one. The realities of both continents may have undergone immense changes, yet the ideas that drive them on have remained quite stable. Americans believe in most of the dreams of the Enlightenment, as well as in their capacity to turn them into reality; Europeans believe in the difficult balancing acts of *Realpolitik*. Americans may very well be on their way to creating a Hobbesian jungle, but they see themselves as servants of universal rights. Europeans might have established a Kantian garden, but they take pride in understating their achievements as much as possible. Hearing them makes one fear that Europe could lose sight of its realities if it does not begin to dream.

The Europeans' refusal to describe themselves in idealistic categories has something to do with the tendency towards self-critique that I praised earlier. Thoughtful Europeans know that standing up for justice at home has only yielded some fruit, and that in other countries it has just produced a few tender buds. One need only take a cheap vacation to Goa to see that the European paradise is based on an international purgatory. When a European explains that her world is still far from ideal, she is in fact standing up for it: Loyalty to an ideal means giving an honest account of how far away it is from being fully realised.

Admittedly, this only explains a small part of the gulf between Americans and Europeans. When Europeans refuse to speak like Kantians, there is a much larger question at stake. Europeans from almost all social classes and countries consider speeches on morality to be slightly embarrassing, and they will therefore be the last to describe the situation in moral terms; yet the awareness that something profound is missing here is just as present among Europeans as among Americans. The words with which they express their admiration for the U.S. may not be as effusive as they were in the 18th century, yet Europeans are drawn to Americans like Obama and Kennedy for the same reasons that they cheered their forefathers Franklin and Paine. It is the appeal of a world that is guided not by the traditions of the past, but rather by visions of the future. They see in the United States a place in which freedom, equality, and possibly also fraternity are instinctual rather than institutional.

Dismissing America's profession to ideals as mere hypocrisy would mean aligning oneself with the reductionist worldview of a Hobbes: Only material conditions are real, and everything else is humbug. This specific conception of reality contains no self-descriptions, dreams, or any of a host of other factors that are essential for the identity of a people and that of their nation. Such dreams and self-descriptions could indeed create new realities; from the perspective of the Old World, the American Revolution was nothing less than a miracle. The Declaration of Independence begins with an opening statement that is, metaphysically speaking, astounding: We hold these truths to be self-evident, that all men are created equal. Even the assertion that only all white men were created equal was anything but obvious; most of the world held it to be, quite simply, false. In 1776, a company of settlers had the audacity to explain the idea of *all* men being equal as self-evident – and to begin to make it true.

Let’s leave reductionism aside and take a look at something else: In Europe, institutions are much more democratic than instincts, while it is just the reverse in America. Americans are democratic from head to toe, while Europeans sing a well-rehearsed and studied song. Nothing against studying, but whoever starts too late with it will probably not get very far, as can be attested to by anyone who has ever seen a European Social Democrat bow and scrape at the sight of a state minister.

American dreams and European realities – that would be a combination worth trying. For Europe will soon forfeit its realities if it does not begin to appreciate them and dream of something new. In the past few decades, sensitive Europeans were prevented from appreciating their considerable achievements by a sense of shame about Europe’s crimes and failures. And the crimes of imperialism make them hesitate to present themselves as a exemplary model. Self-critique, however, is no goal in itself. If it leads to the avoidance of action for fear of making mistakes, then it is much worse than the alternatives. While Europe avidly debates whether it does or does not exist as a whole (and, if it feels like it, confesses its sins), the rest of the world finds itself in a crisis, finds itself seeking new models. Europe is not monolithic, yet when see from the outside it *is* whole. It is not a utopia, but when seen from the outside it is better than the alternatives. Europe provides models for coexistence and diversity, even as it struggles with the accompanying problems; it provides models for the respect of cultures and traditions, even as it redesigns itself; it provides models for protecting the environment; and, finally, for conflict resolution through negotiation instead of bloodshed.

If Europeans believed in themselves, they could play a powerful and productive role in a world that urgently needs them. During the festivities on the occasion of the 50th anniversary of the Treaties of Rome, the official press release contained an 'informational offering' that dealt with questions such as these: 'What does Europe mean for my work?' and 'What advantages does Europe bring me?' Such questions lead us nowhere. Whenever I hear them, I think of John F. Kennedy’s inaugural address: "Ask not what your country can do for you; ask what you can do for your country." Could Europe become an echo of America’s dreams?

The Europe of the New Young Germans[1]

Badr Mohammed

To learn something about Europe – as with every other culture – one must take the time to study its members' insider points of view. Above all, one must examine its members' readiness to participate and the existing possibilities for participation. Europe – just like every culture – is composed of a sum of individuals, of native Europeans and those who moved there from elsewhere. This leads to an examination of the roll of new young Germans in Europe. I developed the concept 'new young Germans' within the framework of an initiative in the year 2000. In order to make use of this concept in the following analysis, I should first describe who the new young Germans actually are.

The 'new' young Germans are a multifaceted group: Extremely different kinds of people can be found therein. People who were born abroad and carry a foreign passport are part of this group, as are their descendants, who are now in the 3rd or 4th generation living in German society. Many were therefore born here, or came here as children and grew up here, or lived the greater part of their lives here. Who should these people feel themselves to be? And who do they want to be? Germans? Migrants? Immigrants?

Germany is an immigration country. According to my definition, an immigration country is characterised by the circumstance that members of different ethnicities, cultures, and religions immigrate to this country and enrich its culture and its people. An *immigration* country must, by its very definition, be shaped by *immigrants*. Yet even in an immigration country, a foundational manifesto determines the framework for the coexistence of cultures: the constitution. This constitution, like the one in the Federal Republic of Germany, protects the existent system, a system of cohesion, yet also one of diversity. All of the following is anchored in the constitution: the freedom of men, the freedom of the sexes, the freedom of culture, and the freedom of religion. Freedom of religion does not mean the freedom to do whatever one wants, but rather means that there exists a freedom to live out one's own religion, one's own understanding of God, as long as this does not involve violating any fundamental rights of one's fellow citizens. The freedom of an individual ends there where the freedom of another individual starts to be limited.

1 Translated from the German by Kareem James Abu-Zeid.

As I said, the constitution facilitates all the conditions needed for the integration of immigrants. Thus, their structural integration is legally guaranteed and can be claimed by any individual. No question about it: The policies fulfil the prerequisites for *structural* integration. Legal security exists through residence visas; and access to education theoretically exists, as well as access to health care and to housing.

Yet is structural integration enough? Must it not necessarily remain a lovely theoretical work if the immigrant does not integrate on the level of identity as well? Identity integration first takes place when immigrants, via healthy patriotism, identify themselves with the society in which they were born and raised. Adopting German citizenship is not enough. One must also commit oneself to acquiring the country's fundamental values, its language, and also its structures. Please do not misunderstand me here! This in no way means that one's mother tongue must be given up. Neither is it necessary for the culture and religion of one's home country to be abandoned. Rather, these are protected and guaranteed via the basic rights of the host society, and they live on alongside the host society's values and norms.

Germany is an immigration country. Many of us are immigrants from many, many countries. With many languages and – I don't mind repeating myself here – cultures and religions. This diversity enriches our society and testifies to its international character, and is in line with the zeitgeist of globalisation. We Germans can proudly walk on the international stage; we can take on the challenges of modernity and together make something of them. This test of our worth should not be seen as something frightening, however. Rather, we must consider it an opportunity for the new German society to mould the diversity and cohesion of the many immigrants who live here through active intercultural and inter-religious dialogue.

We new Germans thus have the opportunity to shape our society ourselves. This is a privilege that is not self-evident when compared to the rest of the world. Let us use this opportunity to shape our society as a chance to plan and organise. Many years have now gone by during which the political and administrative authorities were unable to awaken in the population an awareness of the fact that those people who are characterised – with an upturned nose – as 'foreigners' actually belong to our country. Citizens from immigrant communities are often asked about their relation to German society and the tenor of the answer is generally the same: "We cannot identify with German society." This is a sad and alarming realisation, for German society is indeed also the society of its immigrants; they too are a tile in the great mosaic that is society. Yet these people who I have been sketching are condemned to feel like so-called migrants for their entire lives. This cannot and should not be the meaning of the new German society, for it entails isolation: on the one hand isolation of the new young Germans; yet also the political and administrative authorities' isolating themselves from their responsibilities. Integration is more than the administration of people's files. We cannot permit people like you and me to be reduced to mere numbers and then filed away. The task of the political and administrative authorities is often underestimated; it is laden with responsibility. The integration organised by the state apparatus can only provide secure legal status for someone. The state's involvement in its cultural and religious affairs must be handled with a great amount of intercultural sensitivity. Otherwise the risk of destroying the language, culture, and religion of the immigrant quickly arises, as does the risk of the ultimate destruction of the individual immigrant, who deserves protection. Such a man is not able to identify with Germany and is certainly not able to integrate into its society. Under certain circumstances, he is assimilated or – and this is quite likely the case – he will take up a position of protest, one of separation and segregation, as the Canadian psychologist John Berry has predicted. We can observe the emergence of a parallel society in numerous other countries, and we cannot deny that this process has also begun in Germany. A parallel society within German society threatens both internal peace and the very system of the Federal Republic, a system that we have hitherto rightfully been proud of.

The call for assimilation is thus entirely false, although it sounds temptingly easy. It is a deceptive siren song, as I have attempted to demonstrate. Assimilation seems to be easier than actively dealing with diversity and confronting the risk inherent in integration. Yet I do not want the cultures and religions in Germany to be forced to give up. Adaptation to German culture must not be forced if it is to have any lasting success, i. e. if the immigrant and (above all else) society as a whole are to profit from it. This is the only way for immigrants to bring their desperately needed potential into our society's system. As I have said, intercultural and inter-religious dialogue can only take place voluntarily. Integration can only take place voluntarily. No-one can order it to happen or compel it – anything of this kind would be counterproductive.

This is a short sketch of the problems, or rather – I'd prefer to use a more positive formulation here – the *challenges* that confront the new young Germans. Allow me to tell you about my own voyage of diversity. Since we are an intercultural workshop, a workshop of integration, let me say that we cannot imitate other immigration countries such as the United States of America, Canada, or Australia. Our fate lies in Europe. Let us mould Europe's new intercultural society together. This is what the new young Germans hope for.

The current situation of the new young Germans is simple. Indeed, it is very simple from the point of view of a new young German. On the one hand, there are the 'white' Germans of the majority, and on the other hand there is the minority of the so-called foreigners in the juridical sense. Allow me to briefly clarify a bit of terminology: One began with the term 'foreigner', a term that soon rang hollow and sounded unmodern. Thus, in an effort to stay fashionable, new concepts were found: 'immigrants', 'foreigners with a German passport', 'people with immigrant backgrounds'. Yet as Friedrich Schiller concludes in his poem *Ode an die Freude*, a poem that Ludwig van Beethoven would later set to music: It is not the current outward fashion that will enable men to become brothers. We do not need showy new terms. Eye-catching changes of labels will not help if nothing changes with the situation itself. Pains are taken to reform legislation, laws like the Immigration Law and the Right to Citizenship are passed, yet nothing has changed with the situation of German society, neither then nor now. And why would it? After all, this has, in the meantime, become a profession, both for those 'white' Germans who only tend to their own self-interests and for the so-called labour immigrants. It has become a business in which one can develop many clever projects. Projects that are born on the backs of the weak of our society, people who know nothing about the legal system, the social system, or the system of health care. Who is surprised that these people often fall behind in terms of education and suffer from unemployment, a shortage of housing, and insufficient health care? It is in this social dilemma that prejudices against foreigners arise, ones we know all too well from history. Allow me to say one more thing: We do not have a so-called 'foreigner problem' or 'immigrant problem', but rather – just like all countries – a *social* problem. A social problem, for no ethnicity in the world is intrinsically poor, uneducated, fundamentalist, or criminal. No-one is safe from these social problems, and people from certain social milieus are particularly at risk, independent of their language, their origin, their religion, and their gender. Poverty and wealth both play a role in this social problem. In principle, nothing has changed for centuries: If I immigrate to a country and have money, enough money, then I will be treated differently i. e. courteously by members of the host society. I travel first-class, I live first-class, my doctors are first-rate, I can afford a first-rate legal representative if necessary, and there is a good possibility that my children will be educated beyond merely the first few grades. I am thus privileged in comparison to people who must sleep on the streets with their ten children, whose doctors and lawyers do no more than what is 'required' of them, whose opportunities for education remain limited, and whose status in Germany – often for years on end – is a long series of short-term residence permits.

I do not want to digress from the main topic, so allow me a provocative statement: No, we do not have a problem with foreigners in Germany; we have a problem with Turks. Of course, I do not mean 'the Turkish Problem' that is unfortunately discussed far too often at the beer halls, and that is stirred up by the media and laden with prejudices and stereotypes. No, I mean the following: I mean the fact that an immigrant community has established itself to such an extent that 'white' Germans now have a special lens through which they view all immigrants as Turks. The so-called 'Turkish lens' first of all discriminates against the Turks themselves, for it supports stereotypes and violates – in the figurative sense – their individuality. On the other hand, the Germans, who are used to seeing a Turk in every foreigner, never remove this lens, even when they are dealing with other ethnicities in Germany. One forgets that the era of guest workers ended long ago. And one must *not* forget that the guest workers came not only from Turkey. I can remember many guest workers who came here together and have stayed here together, for example Italians, Greeks, people from former Yugoslavia, Vietnamese, Tunisians, Moroccans, and many others. As long as policies are made only for those of Turkish descent, and as long as – because of the Turkish lens – people do not realise that other immigrants and their descendants live here as well, there will be conflict with the largest immigrant group. No, let me correct myself: The group of Turkish descent is not actually the largest immigrant group. Consider our Germans of Russian or Polish descent, or people from former Yugoslavia. As long as the conflict between immigrants of Turkish descent and 'white' Germans continues in this way, we will be able to amend the new German society only with great difficulty. What we new Germans want is the recognition and acknowledgement of all the Germans who live here. At the moment, it is only our German citizenship that allows us to be identified as Germans. Our struggle for equal opportunities as German citizens within our society is only possible with mutual respect and a cooperative dialogue where we are on equal footing with one another. Equal opportunities are not possible if we are eternally branded as immigrants. Of course, conflicts are not easy to resolve, but if there is no political will and no willingness to acknowledge other groups, then all attempts at a solution are condemned to failure from the outset, and it will be difficult for us to prepare the new German society for the 21st century. Therefore, we new young Germans call for the integration of all immigrants living here as well as for multilateral structures and organisation, and not for the lobbying of a minority. The majority of new young Germans feel discriminated against and underrepresented. Integration and the incorporation of diversity into German society can only succeed through multilateral relations with the many nationalities, cultures, and religions in Germany. The bridge between us Germans must be erected within Germany. We will only be able to describe ourselves as an exemplary immigration country and show our face in the international arena by first dealing with our diversity in a conscious fashion and striving for better integration policies. So, back to the nation's household tasks! If we want to work on a German nation that is supposed to consist of many nationalities, cultures, and religions, we must stop focusing on only one ethnic group and ignoring all the others.

In addition, we immigrants must recognise Germany as our homeland and begin to describe ourselves as German-Turks, German-Kurds, German-Arabs, German-Russians, German-Vietnamese, and so forth. We all share a common constitution; we do not have one constitution for German-Turks, another one for German-Russians, and yet another one for German-Arabs. This is the only way for us Germans of diverse origins to foster a healthy German patriotism. It is abundantly clear that we new young Germans are in need of this patriotism, that we want to engage ourselves with our homeland and to identify ourselves with it. At the Football World

Cup two years ago, German-Turks and German-Russians together cheered on the German-Polish Lukas Podolski's goals and the German-Ghanaian David Odonkor's sprints up the flank, and they all listened with their arms around each other to the music of the multinational singer Xavier Naidoo. Even if, as the composer himself formulated, "*dieser Weg wird kein leichter sein*" ("this way will not be an easy one"), the generation of new young Germans hopes for a coexistence that is marked by friendly ties.

Apropos of friendly ties: Do you know how many mixed marriages there are? We are beginning to love one another. My relationship is only one example of this: My wife is Greek; she is European. I am of Kurdish descent. My children are many things: Greek, Kurdish, German, Indo-Germanic. In a word: They are Europeans. We Germans are not alone. We are not the only ones faced with these challenges. All 27 nations of the European Union are faced with them, some to a lesser extent, some to a greater extent. It is thus not possible for the discussion about European integration to take place from the perspective of non-Europeans, for 'non-European' is an erroneous label: All people living in Europe, all individuals who have a part in European society have the right to take call themselves 'European', regardless of their language, culture, and religion.

This is no different from my previously formulated thesis about the new young Germans. As in Germany, in the European Union many children of international *and* European descent are being born. As a European, I can only say: I do *not* feel like a non-European.

I am coming to the conclusion: We new young Germans simply hope for three things:

First, we hope for integration to be more than a simple residence permit. Access to education and work, healthcare and housing is also a part of integration. And we hope that all these rights continue to remain untouched and anchored in the German and European constitutions.

Second, we hope for all of us to be given the opportunity to preserve our language, our culture, and our religion. We hope that the administrative and political authorities consciously decide against assimilation strategies and recognise that voluntary action is the best motivator for integration.

Third, we hope that an open inter-religious and intercultural dialogue will take place, one in which all individuals are able to have their say, regardless of their origins, language, religion, sex, or the colour of their skin. And we hope that all immigrant groups will be recognised and all distorting (figurative) lenses set aside, so that the clientelism of individual (immigrant) lobbies will be put to an end.

If these wishes are granted, the conditions will be ripe for the new young Germans to also actually feel like Germans. The seed that is beginning to sprout from this fertile ground gives me the courage to hope that the new young Germans and the new young Europeans will be exemplars for a united Europe, a Europe that consists of many nations and cultures – and not only those that are 'genuinely' European. These new young Germans and Europeans are inviting *all* Europeans to proclaim: "My continent is Europe!"

Europe and Its Foreigners. From Eurocentrism to Multiculturalism[1]

Ralph Ghadban

European Colonial Rule

The great discoveries of the 15th century set into motion a process of internationalisation by linking the different continents together. Since then, a world market has arisen, one which – after the Industrial Revolution – was first labelled 'capitalist', and is called 'global' today. The history of humanity thus became a common history.

The Europeans were not aware that they were, with their discoveries, bringing the entire world into modernity. Vasco da Gama and Christopher Columbus pursued primarily mercantilist goals, as did the countless commercial companies that were established thereafter and that were active across the world. After the Industrial Revolution, the world became more closely connected through a capitalist world market. The monopolies inevitably fell; the commercial companies lost their privileges. Direct rule was necessary to secure provision of raw materials for the home countries' industries.

Starting in 1880, the expansion of direct colonial rule became a race among the European powers for the dividing up of the world. Empires arose. At the beginning of the 20th century, colonial regions covered a third of the earth's surface. Out of a total world population of two billion people, 700 million – and within that 160 million from a total of 200 million Muslims – lived under direct European rule. With the emergence of these empires, Eurocentrism began to catch on.

At the beginning of the 19th century, Kant spoke in the spirit of the Enlightenment about the human species, saying that every man is entitled to the use of reason. For Hegel, in contrast, only Europe embodied the historical subject, one that would complete world history. Asia had fulfilled its historical role and was thus finished as a historical subject. Africa was never even able to fulfil this function, because it remained at a standstill on the threshold of world history.[2] Joseph Arthur Graf von Gobineau's race theory and Herbert Spencer's social Darwinism perfected the ideological construct of Eurocentrism.

1 Translated from the German by Kareem James Abu-Zeid.

2 *Hegel, Georg Wilhelm Friedrich*: Vorlesungen über die Theorie der Geschichte, Frankfurt am Main 1970, p. 129.

Eurocentric ideas informed colonial theory and colonial praxis. The policy of co-operation replaced the policy of assimilation that had, under the influence of the French Revolution, aimed for the total integration of all men in a civil society. The French had attempted this in Algeria without success. By contrast, the policy of cooperation abandoned attempts at modernising the 'traditional' societies, as it called them. It contented itself with setting up a modern sector alongside the traditional one in order to enable the exploitation of a country's resources with the help of its indigenous peoples. This slim modern sector included education, administration, the military, and an economic infrastructure for the exploitation of raw materials. Those who took part in this were recruited from the elite, and some of them were educated in the European home countries. Those were the 'assimilable' ones. The rest fell under the rubric of 'traditional' and were generally divided along tribal lines. They were thus in no position to establish a nation-state. The traditional society is a segmented society that stands outside of history.

European Identity

After the Second World War, Europeans brought in millions of workers from the colonies, or rather the former colonies, in order to rebuild their destroyed countries. The immigrants posed new challenges to Europe that were not foreseeable. The Europeans became aware of these challenges far too late because they never had – and still do not have – any effective immigration policies. The ethnic self-understanding of the European peoples was challenged, as were its religions and the humanistic traditions that inform its historical identity. The recent debates about Turkey's entry into the EU as well as the European Constitution show quite clearly to what extent the cultural identity of the Europeans has begun to waver. To this day, it remains unclear whether it is Christianity alone or Christianity together with the Enlightenment that makes up Europe's identity, or whether Christianity is even a part of that identity at all. On the other hand, it is even less clear whether an Islamic country that is not even situated in Europe can become a part of Europe. The leader of the Anglican Church's call, a few months ago, for elements of the sharia to be introduced into Great Britain quite clearly shows how unstable this cultural identity has become.

1. Immigration

The industrial nations first supplied themselves with labour from the lesser developed countries of southern Europe, until these southern countries themselves experienced an economic upturn and sought their own immigrant workers. With the emergence of the European Community (EC) and the expansion of the European Union (EU) to include almost all of Europe, European immigrants gained a predominantly European identity that facilitated their integration into the respective states.

The booming economy craved more workers, workers who often came from the former colonies and were predominantly Muslims. The countries without (former) colonies 'helped themselves' mainly to workers from Islamic recruitment countries around the Mediterranean. Germany alone, which after the building of the Wall in 1961 no longer received workers from the DDR, facilitated the entry of over one and a half million Muslims in the 1960's. This was done via recruitment agreements with Turkey in 1961, Morocco in 1963, Tunisia in 1965, and Yugoslavia in 1968.

In the years 1973-74, the recruitment of foreign workers was halted in all of Europe because of economic reasons. The result of this was that immigrants, due to restrictions on their own freedom of movement, had their families come to them. In this way, several million more Muslims arrived in Europe in the 1970's within the framework of reuniting families. In the 1980's and 1990's, it was mainly Muslim refugees from Turkey, Iraq, Iran, Lebanon, and Afghanistan, as well as from the Balkans, Bosnia, Albania, and Kosovo, who found shelter in Western Europe. The number of Muslims in the European Union is estimated at 17 to 20 million, of which 3.2 million live in Germany. There are no exact numbers due to the lack of statistical surveys on denominations in the European countries.

Europe's inadequate immigration policies have since only made noticeable progress with regards to security. Within the framework of the Schengen Agreement, numerous laws were passed as protective measures. On the other hand, apart from a few exceptions, these policies did not develop any concept of integration. They reckoned with the return of the immigrants to their countries of origin. 'Lower' unqualified jobs were assigned to third world immigrants, who were housed in poor neighbourhoods and whose participation in the social, cultural, and political diversity of society was limited. Thus, in the 1950's and 60's there was talk of an 'ethnoclass', and in the 70's of *Unterschichtung*, i. e. the creation of an underclass; both terms demonstrate the inferior position of immigrant workers at the lowest rungs of the social scale, in a process that was equivalent to a ghettoisation.

This dominance further confirmed the supposed civilisational superiority of the Europeans. They demanded total adaptation on the part of the migrants, without however being supportive of this. They were very convinced of the integrational power of democracy as a superior civilisational model. Basic needs of the immigrants, such as learning the native language and practicing their own religion, as well as political participation and representation – which incidentally in no way contradict the demands of civilisation – were not taken into consideration. In the name of a more-or-less ethnically homogenous nation-state, the immigrants' incorporation into the existing structures was required – a kind of assimilation, from which in fact only a few could profit because of the lack of necessary integrational measures. The overwhelming majority of immigrants were refused the opportunity to integrate. It was said that their traditional pre-modern orientation was an essential characteristic of their ethnic affiliation and could not easily be shaken off. The immigrants were ethnicised in the negative sense. One need only think back to the discussion in the 1980's of the integrational capacity of the Turks in Germany to see this.

This basically racist slant of policies in the European home countries was in itself a continuation of the racist policies in the colonies – with the difference that the third world peoples were no longer subject to the arbitrary acts of the colonial administration, but rather were subject to the state under the rule of law. This state proved itself to be their main ally. With its help, the immigrants solidified their residence, gained equal status with the native Europeans, and fought against discriminating and exclusionary immigration policies. Across Europe, these policies have two main thrusts: There is the policy of assimilation and the policy of cooperation. The first belongs to countries such as France and Germany, the second to countries such as Great Britain and Holland.

The first immigration law in Great Britain, 'The Nationality Act' of 1948, was very liberal and encouraged immigration. The immigrants came in the 1950's as citizens of the Commonwealth and attained British citizenship through registration. They became citizens with rights to vote, and without being required to integrate. This was a normal process, because citizenship in Great Britain does not mean belonging to a state based on nationality, but rather belonging to a state with several nationalities: Scots, Welsh, Irish, and Englishmen. The British system seeks no assimilation of its citizens, but rather favours a juxtaposition of political identities. In this way, the Afro-Caribbeans, the Indians, the Pakistanis, and the Bangladeshis built up their closed societies without any trouble.

In the Netherlands, the pillar system establishes the freedom of education. This means that, alongside the neutral state schools, confessional schools with 100 % state financing are allowed to exist and are not subject to any state supervision. The pillar system includes not only education, but also welfare, hospitals, and the media. Out of consideration for the general good, the state is entitled to support religious groups in building and maintaining their infrastructures. Islam was treated as a new pillar of the system, and thus the Muslims – Turks and Moroccans – could build up their closed societies with the help of the state. In both countries, structural incorporation of Muslims was realised, yet social and political integration did not take place due to both latent and open racism.

In France and Germany, structural incorporation is out of the question; only individual integration to the point of assimilation is possible. In France, a public immigration policy was begun in 1945 with the founding of the 'Office national de l'immigration' (ONI). It was not only to cover the need for workers, but also to offset the chronic demographic weaknesses of the country through the permanent settlement of immigrants. In the second half of the 1950's the economy began to circumvent the immigration system by recruiting illegal workers in a big way. There were the 'clandestins', who worked illegally and were paid less than minimum wage. The percentage of illegals with respect to total immigration reached 53 % in 1960, and further increased in the following years (69 % in 1964, 79 % in 1967, 82 % in 1968), reaching 90 % in 1973. Illegal immigration became the immigration norm. Poorly paid and without any assistance from the state, the immigrants gathered in the poor neighbourhoods of city suburbs, known as 'banlieus', which have become hotbeds of social unrest and, due to the large percentage of Muslims, have shaped the face of Islam in France.

In Germany, mass immigration began late, starting in 1961. Before this, fourteen million German exiles, re-settlers, and emigrants had come into the country and been integrated. Yet the political authorities did not want to integrate the non-German immigrants, the so-called guest workers. A policy of rotation was pursued whereby workers were replaced annually. But this was quickly undermined by the economy due to the costs of training new workers. The guest workers' periods of stay were extended, their numbers grew, yet an integration policy was still nowhere in sight. Until 1998, and despite the presence of circa eight million foreigners, the official line was that Germany was not an immigration country. A bare-bones immigration law first came into force in early 2005.

In all countries, the political authorities bet on the integrational power of society, and especially that of work. It seemed that integration through work was inevitable, yet two processes thwarted the politicians' plans. The first was the process of the creation of an underclass: the immigrant workers were incorporated into the lowest functional levels of the economic system and took physically demanding jobs that required no qualifications – they worked for the most part at conveyor belts in the factories. In 1960's Germany, for example, two million German workers were promoted to salaried employees and left their working-class jobs to the guest workers. The second process began with the restructuring of the working world as a result of the revolution in information technology, which led to increased efficiency of production. Starting in the mid-70's, robots gradually replaced workers on the conveyor belts, and unemployment has steadily risen ever since. In 2005, unemployment in Germany as a whole was at 11.7 %, in Berlin at 18.5 %, among Turkish Berliners at 48.5 %, and among Arab Berliners at over 90 %.

The integration of immigrants, who were overwhelmingly Muslim, had failed everywhere in Europe. In the 1980's, people began to speak of identity politics and multiculturalism. There were hopes of holding together the society that was drifting apart via a policy of recognition. This was supposed to offset the lacking material integration policies.

2. Multiculturalism

Parallel to the demise of the notion of work as an integrational force, racism and discrimination – due to their exclusionary power – played an important role in the emergence of multiculturalism in all countries. In the 1950's and 60's, left-wing and liberal Europeans joined in solidarity with the independence movements in the third world. They viewed the immigrant ethno-class in their home countries as an ally against the capitalist system. The integration of the immigrants would thus depend on the result of the working-class struggle. In the 1970's, they fought the ideological hegemony of Eurocentrism and advocated the rights of ethnic minorities in Europe. They called for a multiethnic and multicultural society. By the end of the 1980's, multiculturalism had prevailed almost everywhere in Europe.

Public – that is to say, violent – displays of xenophobia began in Great Britain in the 1960's, in France in the 1970's, and in Germany in the 1980's. In Holland, non-violent racism was so effective that in 1983 the government officially adopted a multicultural policy, which led to even more disintegration because it reinforced the structures of recognised pre-existing communities, and thus threatened society with communitarian fragmentation. Communitarianism aims at the division of society into different religious and ethnic communities. This division allows the various groups to preserve their identity and way of life. In 1994, the Dutch government officially abandoned its multicultural policy and began to foster shared values instead of differences.

In Great Britain, the breakthrough of multiculturalism with the 'Race Relations Act' of 1976 had already led to the establishment of a commission for race equality, through which minority identities were institutionalised. From 1979 to 1997, the conservatives in power pushed through multicultural policies that led to communitarian developments and thus even deeper fragmentation of society. The Labour Party, which came into power in 1997, openly held to multicultural policies, and today is one of the few governments in all of Europe that still adheres to such policies.

In Germany and France, multicultural policies were practised in roundabout ways, if not officially then certainly de facto. The Association Law of 1981, which was amended in 1987, abolished state control in France and thus paved the way for the emergence of numerous Islamic associations and improved their financial strength. Through a French peculiarity that considers religion to be a part of the general culture, it was possible to have the secular state finance religious associations. These associations, which were controlled by Islamists, played a decisive role in the radicalisation and Islamisation of disadvantaged second-generation immigrants.

In Germany, where a policy of exclusion was still being practised, the second generation turned to ideologies that emphasised their isolation. They found these ideologies among Islamists who presented their religion as a means of creating an identity. Because of the special status of religion in the German Constitution, the immigrants and their children gained recognition as Muslims, something which had been denied them until now as simple citizens. In the 1990's, inter-religious dialogue blossomed. The state institutions granted ever-increasing recognition to the Islamic Mosque Organisations and Associations and kindly allowed them to undertake some of the state institutions' tasks. Just as happened in France, parts of education, upbringing, social work, and sporting activities came under the responsibility of these associations, which to a large extent were under the influence of Islamists. They were able to propagate an ideology of hate against the West, and also a way of living that collided in many respects with the Western democratic state under the rule of law. Thus, in both countries, so-called parallel societies emerged, societies which had their own values and which offered an alternate way of life. They are different from the communitarian groups in Great Britain and Holland in that they do not enjoy any institutional recognition, yet in terms of content and function they are similar. Both countries, Germany and France, have since distanced themselves from multiculturalism.

The multiculturalist policies based on the struggle against racism and discrimination damned and discredited the European identity, and relativised its universal values. Werner Schiffauer, an advocate of multiculturalism, wrote the following as late as 2003, a time when the disintegrating effects of these policies were already visible everywhere:

> "Ist es nicht gerade die in diesem Zusammenhang immer beschworene christlich-abendländische Wertegemeinschaft, aus der heraus der Massenmord an Juden verursacht wurde und auf deren Kappe Kolonialismus, Imperialismus und Rassismus entstanden sind, die nun im Namen der Demokratie ihnen [den Muslimen] moralische Bekenntnisse abverlangt?"[3]

Because of their historical guilt, Europeans are apparently no longer allowed to make these demands on Muslims. Even the last bastion of the Europeans, the nation-state, disintegrated – its end was announced in the 1990's. In the age of globalisation, the nation-state is no longer able to deliver answers to economic, social, and political questions. Under these circumstances, the communitarian segmentation of European cities would correspond to the tribal segmentation of the third world colonies.

3 "Is not that very same Christian-Western community of values which is constantly evoked in this context, and which caused the genocide of the Jews and was responsible for the emergence of colonialism, imperialism, and racism – is it not that which now, in the name of democracy, demands professions of allegiance from [the Muslims]?"; *Schiffauer, Werner*: Das Schweigen am Rande, in: TAZ, 30. 01. 2003, p. 12.

The multicultural ideology has also spread in the Muslim secular camp. For example, the Turkish Association in Berlin-Brandenburg (TBB) considers Germany a polyethnic state and calls for the following:

> "Alle Menschen in Deutschland sollen die kulturelle Diversität der deutschen Gemeinschaft anerkennen, reflektieren und ihr entgegenkommen."[4]

There follows a list of rights that, curiously, extend beyond Germany's borders:

> "Die Rechte von Menschen, die aus ökonomischen, sozialen, ökologischen und anderen Gründen zum Verlassen ihrer Heimat gezwungen sind und in die Bundesrepublik Deutschland einwandern wollen, müssen im Rahmen eines neuen 'Einwanderungsgesetzes' geregelt werden."[5]

The state would not even have a say in determining the annual quota of immigrants:

> "Die jährlichen Quoten und Staaten werden durch eine unabhängige Institution festgesetzt, in der gesellschaftliche Institutionen, UNCHR und EinwandererInnenorganisationen beteiligt werden."[6]

Immigrants will recruit other immigrants. The interests of the state, to say nothing of the interests of the European peoples, are not mentioned anywhere.

Multiculturalism has doubtlessly contributed to a greater understanding and acceptance of foreigners, yet in many cases it has also led to extreme forms of tolerance that are not always easy to comprehend. This typically European tolerance happened at a time when, following the 1979 Iranian Revolution, Islamism was on the advance and was being adopted by the children and grandchildren of first-generation immigrants as an ideology that offered an alternate identity to the rejected European one. Islamic identity emphasises belonging to a community of Muslims, to the Umma, and provides an increased feeling of self-worth: Islam is the true religion and it is Muslims who constitute the best community – in contrast to the decadent, corrupt, and amoral West. Islamocentrism thus takes the place of Eurocentrism.

---

4 "All people in Germany should recognise the cultural diversity of German society, reflect on it, and accommodate it."; *Türkischer Bund in Berlin-Brandenburg*: Gleichstellungspolitik statt Ausländerpolitik, October 1999; http://www.tbb-berlin.de [15. 10. 2010].

5 "The rights of people who are forced to abandon their homes and who want to immigrate to Germany – whether due to economic, social, ecological, or other reasons – should be laid down within the framework of a new 'Immigration Law'."; ibid.

6 "The states and annual quotas will be determined by an independent institution in which social institutions, the UNCHR, and internal immigrant organisations take part."; ibid.

Conclusion

The road from Eurocentrism to multiculturalism was quite short. Both approaches drove people apart, mishandled the values of the Enlightenment, and increased the potential for conflict in European societies. It is high time that we reflect on our democratic pluralism in order to seek what unites rather than what divides us. We must come to understand the slogan of the multiculturalists – the right to difference, '*le droit à la différence*' – as an expression of individual freedom on the common basis of human rights, and not as the inherent right of cultural groups, regardless of whether these groups are of a religious or an ethnic nature.

References

Hegel, Georg Wilhelm Friedrich: Vorlesungen über die Theorie der Geschichte, Frankfurt am Main 1970

Schiffauer, Werner: Das Schweigen am Rande, in: TAZ, 30. 01. 2003, p. 12

Türkischer Bund in Berlin-Brandenburg: Gleichstellungspolitik statt Ausländerpolitik, October 1999; http://www.tbb-berlin.de [15. 10. 2010]

Remarks on Culture and Diversity[1]

Anil Bhatti

In discussions about culture and diversity perspective plays an important role. The view from India need not necessarily be the same as from other parts of the world and how I look on pluricultural relations this time, need not necessarily be the same as from elsewhere. This struck me first when I saw a map of the world which was projected from the point of New Zealand. And the globe looked completely different. This unsettling experience is the basis from which, I think, discussions in culture studies should start. It is a kind of strategic unsettling of hitherto settled notions. And this is also the way in which I think we could consider some of the topics of the 11th Karlsruhe Dialogues.

It seems to me, that discussing culture and diversity implies a discussion about what I may call "renegotiation of the coordinates of life world." Questions of power, freedom or autonomy are involved. The tension between old and new, between continuity and rupture leads to various kinds of anxieties and these are not the same everywhere and they do not arise out of the same reasons everywhere. Some things work in one place and do not work elsewhere. The degree to which I am disturbed by the strange and alien and the uncanny varies. How much strangeness or alienness can I tolerate? Skin colour for instance or physiognomy may not seem to be a public problem in a particular country, but religion is and similarly on the other hand in another part of the world religion is not so important, but skin colour is very important. In some parts of the world plurality of languages is normal. Elsewhere tensions based on the relationship between language and power are characteristic in the socio-political framework. We can thus have different types of problems based on religious fundamentalism or racism or language and very often these can overlap.

Could the basic problem simply be: When does something look out of place and when does it stop looking out of place? And who determines this? I suggest this in the context to what might be called two basic models of looking at the problems of culture in what may loosely be called the post-colonial-world in a temporal and conceptual sense of the term. This term refers to the fact that we theorize after the historical end of colonialism but that our way of thinking nevertheless continuously and constantly incorporates and reflects through the colonial historical para-

---

1 This text is the revised version of my presentation at the 11th Karlsruhe Dialogues. I have tried to retain the character of a spoken presentation. Earlier remarks on these questions have been published as *Anil Bhatti*: Kulturelle Vielfalt und Homogenisierung, in: *Johannes Feichtinger* et al. (ed.): Habsburg Postcolonial. Machtstrukturen und kollektives Gedächtnis, Innsbruck et al. 2003, p. 55-68; *ibid.*: Diversität und Homogenisierung, in: Diskussionsforum: Postkoloniale Arbeiten/Postcolonial Studies; www.goethezeitportal.de/index.php?id=1431 [15. 10. 2010].

digm. The first model emphasizes what may be called 'the loss of authenticity', the progressive loss of authenticity through colonialism. In this model we are constantly trying to recover our roots, we are constantly trying to find a genuine way of life. This leads in my opinion – and I cut short the argument – to what you might call 'closed visions of culture'. Different cultures are conceived as monads, as closed systems. These systems interact with each other, collide as Eric Wolf suggested like billiard balls, but they do not necessarily open up by dissolving their protective outer covering. Relations between these closed entities or monads are constructed as if they were independent units with separate stable identities.

The other model emphasizes interconnectedness and overlapping histories. The modern post Columbian world is an interconnected world in which deeper and deeper forms of interconnections are developing, histories are being shared. Colonial conquest and anti colonial liberation, discovery and migration all strengthen this enmeshment so that there is no such thing as static, unalloyed authenticity. We are constantly living in situations of flux with permeable surfaces and porous boundaries in which lines of solidarities are established across cultures and the reasons why they are established and the forms in which they are established can always be discussed at every moment of the process. From this perspective cultures are fluid and not bounded. We do not have closed essentialised cultural units reacting to each other. Rather, we have mobile, shifting areas of overlapping interests.

The above remarks lead me to the next consideration. In the present international situation one may see two tendencies: on the one hand relatively homogeneous societies are moving towards complex formations and I look upon the process of the formation of Europe as a formation in which relatively homogeneous societies – one language, one religion, a relatively clear territorial boundary – are coming together to become a rather complex, an alarmingly diverse society with many languages, at least three major religions, maybe more (who knows) and territorial ambiguities. Now, of course we know that, shall we say Germany is not a completely homogenous country: you have religious diversity and everybody who has been to the south of Germany and to the north of Germany knows that there are regional specificities and antipathies, but nevertheless Germany is not as diverse as India. India has the kind of sub-continental diversity which Europe is gradually, consciously accepting. We have in India 22 official languages, all major religions and many smaller religions, all the races, all accumulated in this rather puzzling state called India. The significant fact is that such complex formations like India are subjected to the pressures of various fundamentalist tendencies, which I call "tendencies towards homogenization" as the second present tendency. The fabric of Indian society and Indian culture which was based on the presence of many languages, the presence of many religions and a peculiar form of fluid syncretistic culture is increasingly broken by homogeneous tendencies which privilege either the language or the religion or a certain territory as forming the basis or the authentic way of organizing society. That is the important point. The important demand is that society must be organized in such a way that you have discrete, separated entities which can be managed or governed in a separated manner. They cohere by an appeal to either a language or a religion or territorial contiguity or a supposedly common privileged history. All this in the singular respectively and each by definition special as far as the demand is concerned. The history is invented, like most histories, and it typically refers to a golden age which was destroyed by the entry of extraneous forces which are held responsible for the detested heterogeneous structure of the present.

In many ways the tendency towards homogenization is a continuation of a model proposed in the 19th century and it goes back to one of the greatest thinkers of the 19th century, Johann Gottfried Herder, who starts a very interesting reflection on Europe in his *Ideen zu einer Philosophie der Geschichte der Menschheit*, by pointing out that Europe is the result of an extraordinary mixing of races and cultures. Europe emerged out of a chaotic beginning. There is no such thing as a pure authentic European origin. But precisely because of this primeval mixture the task in Europe became one of organizing itself into smaller entities which have a contiguity of language, history and territory because this corresponds to the divine plan of nature. Mixed societies are unnatural societies. The natural society is then supposedly the society in which everything is as contiguous as possible and the features required for ensuring contiguity are usually language, religion, territory, and a postulated common history or myth. This, incidentally, also explains why Herder was against colonialism. Herder's writings are full of anti-colonial sentiments, because he thinks that colonialism is in fact an attempt to mix up and muddle the natural situation of the world. It is best to leave the world as it is, as a collection of uncluttered, segregated units, each of which has their own different track of history and logic of development. Colonialism from the Herderian perspective is a violent interference in the autonomous paths of development of separate, autonomous cultures. There is no room in Herder's thought for the kind of awareness of complex interconnected world historical processes which forms the basis of Goethe's notion of emerging World Literature.

It is against the background of this ideology of a so-called natural pre-existent order, that we understand the typical tendency in colonialism which is then to break up existing multilingual, pluricultural, multireligious societies by classifying them into smaller, singular units. One of the great enterprises in this direction of reducing complexity, the linguistic survey of India in the late 19th century, broke up entire regions of communication where there was a practical tradition of linguistic communication through travel and trade into separated languages. Once these languages were invented and were separated out of a linguistic continuum and were given codified grammars of their own, they developed the eternal dynamics of actually becoming different, retaining their difference, maintaining their own interest in remaining different and this broke up a huge continuum of communicative territory into segregated units with firm boundaries. This drive – and this drive is the 19th century drive, it is a colonialist drive, it is a drive which is part of modern scientific, analytic, taxonomic energies – was inherited as a problem in the entire process of decolonization by having a paradigm of either a homogeneous, contiguous state based on religion or language or territory or, on the other hand, a pluricultural, heterogeneous, secular state.

I use the word 'pluricultural' rather than the established term 'multicultural' because there is a conceptual difference. Multiculturalism in the established version of the term essentialises cultures and then allows them to exist with separated boundaries and with their own internal dynamics. As a result, you can have a ghetto-like situation – different cultures in a society – in which the problems of hierarchy, exploitation, human bondage within these cultures is left to them, it is their internal business, what they do inside their houses is not our business. That is multiculturalism. Now, pluriculturalism does not accept walls and boundaries of this kind. Pluricultural societies create situations where people from different backgrounds come together and establish conditions for making it possible for them to come together. So pluriculturalism actually is based on breaking down the walls between cultures while accepting the fact of diversity. This is the crucial epistemological point: walls are breaking down, but diversity is maintained. And this is what pluriculturalism implies. – The emphasis on pluriculturalism is a way of opposing the essentialisation of parallel cultures in the same society.

The secular state is a state in which it is possible to imagine that the viability of socio-political organisation can create a public space in which the language I speak, the religion I profess or the history I appeal to can coexist provided I respect one criterion – that is of generating a pragmatic habitus in which the fact of getting along with each other is more important than understanding each other. In complex societies it is not necessary to burden our social lives with the imperative of hermeneutics of understanding difference. It is more important in complex societies to cultivate the interest in the art of getting along with each other and deferring the moment of interpretation and understanding. This implies that we respect and recognize a certain norm of interpersonal behavior as the basis for which is the constitution incorporating some vision of a tolerant society or some vision of a pluricultural society. Whichever constitutional framework we want to adopt, we envisage a society in which it is possible to be different without necessarily excluding the other. And this difference between what you might call the homogenous state, the postcolonial homogenous state, and the heterogeneous secular state was captured in my opinion with an evocative image by Nehru, when he talked of India as a cultural palimpsest. Cultures are palimpsests. A palimpsest is a term common in history, especially the history of art and it refers to manuscripts which are constantly overwritten. Palimpsests are surfaces where layers are painted over to provide us with new pictures. Ultimately you have many layers of writing or of paint on the parchment or the canvas. But the crucial point is that this parchment is a totality, no layer of which can be called the authentic Ur-layer. All the layers are conditioned by each other and they belong together. The moment you say that of the ten layers that exist, only layer number three is authentic, you are a fundamentalist, because then you want to remove all the other layers, you want to erase them. So in my view fundamentalism is the theory of eraser in culture leading to violence, terror, racism which I think all of us know about from our contemporary political history. This image of culture as palimpsest was also used by Victor Hugo to characterize Europe and it has been used very often by many thinkers who want to look upon culture not necessarily as something born fully developed from some spring, but as something that evolves over time and which is a complex negotiable category with many affiliations in time and space.

I think this is a very important term for my way of thinking: cultures are negotiable processes. They should not necessarily be looked upon as authentic given quantities right from the beginning. They emerge out of time, out of complex processes and out of complex histories. They generate what is known as 'shared memories'. The concept of 'shared memories' is an important aspect of the discussion about culture. The palimpsestic society in contrast to the fundamentalist society is an inclusive society. The other type of fundamentalist societies are excluding societies, they exclude you either because you have a different skin colour or you have a different religion or you do not speak the same language or you do not have the same history. In an inclusive society difference is not crucial provided one accepts what may be called a contract of living together on the basis of an agreed norm of what I personally would call 'enlightenment thinking' or a certain kind of a tolerant thinking which is there in all parts of the world, in Europe, in the East and all parts of the globe.

If one could think of a comparative history of tolerance, one would see how similar the notion of tolerance is to all cultures. It is a notion which can be reduced to very small principles. Unfortunately very few societies want to accept small simple principles; they prefer larger notions which imply grand solutions and grand disasters.

One of the features of an inclusive, heterogeneous society is first of all, that it resists clear definition. In a fuzzy way you muddle through the complex problems of this kind of a society. And, incidentally, the German equivalent of 'muddling through' would be *fortwurschteln*. This was a term which was used for the cultural situation of the Habsburg Empire and Robert Musil's ironic chapter on Kakanien speaks about this in *Der Mann ohne Eigenschaften*. And that was precisely the way in which the Habsburg Empire dealt with the enormous differences in language, territorial history and cultures. And as you know, the Empire broke up at least partly because of the emergence of a nationalist ideology based on the Herderian understanding that basically the only way to have authentic culture is to have contiguous territories with their own languages and religions separated each other.

Now to proceed from this to the question of whether you want to be a federation of autonomous cultural units or whether you want to become separate national units with your own flag is a very small step. The Austro-Marxists grappled with this problem and their ideas are still relevant for the discussion about the tension between nationalist aspirations in large complex societies and the transnational idea. This was a discussion which also played an important role in the anti-colonial movement and some of Tagore's remarks after the First World War on the question of nationalism and transnationalism are remarkably relevant even today. But that apart – in our present discussion, I only wanted to emphasize the notion of not having a very clearly defined bounded system of organization.

Large, inclusive societies are also multilingual societies, because they include people with different heritages and languages as part of the common heritage. As far as languages are concerned I should add – maybe, very briefly – that the question of language diversity has been debated so often and it is so much part of discussions on Europe that I only briefly mention why it seems that here some closer attention to Indian experience may be helpful. The Indian experience of pluricultural multilingualism and language diversity is very difficult to define. You cannot capture it with the traditional behaviorist model of code-switching. A multilingual situation is one in which the multilingual speaker has a repertoire, just as a musician has a repertoire which he can unfold, which he can use appropriately and he can move in this repertoire like a musician who improvises on an instrument. And this is what puzzles people who come from monolingual backgrounds, when they see how an Indian conversation progresses in which many languages are used simultaneously. The monolingual listener finds this confusing and wonders how this is done. And this is precisely the point, because if you are playing music, nobody would wonder, why you glide from one *Tonlage* to another. This and this is precisely what you do in a multilingual situation. This is how they function.

There is a very important epistemological consequence here. A North Indian with Hindi as a 'mother tongue' (a problematic notion) does not look upon Tamil – which is in South India – as a foreign language. It is just another Indian language. From an Indian point of view the notion of foreign languages becomes relevant when one looks upon other parts of the globe. One then discovers that French and German or Japanese or Chinese or other languages are part of our global experience. In Europe at present one still looks upon other European languages as foreign languages rather than as just other European languages. One still looks upon them as foreign languages which are part of *Fremdsprachenunterricht*. Now, this may sound a bit peculiar, but I think that the relationships between languages in a multilingual situation are very different from the relationships between languages in unilingual situations with monocultural entities which are part of a federal unity. Again we have this fuzzy notion of boundaries and borders in languages, which allow you moments of transition between languages and other languages – without necessarily claiming the right to say that either of them is privileged. This is why one of the basic conditions for multilingual situations is that it is not necessary to know every language very well – you only should know it well enough to use it. The whole pedagogical drive towards perfectionism in language is against multilingualism. What you have to do is reduce the level of competency required in language-use in order to create multilingual societies and leave the specialization and perfecting then to a later situation. Large urban configurations have these possibilities. Europe also had them. I am reminded of the ironic phrase coined by the Austrian writer Heimito von Doderer who spoke of the "*polyglotte Bereitschaft*" of Vienna. A kind of readiness to be polyglot. Urban societies develop this ability to tolerate large numbers of languages which are spoken, some well, some not well. This sounds like confusion to people brought up in monolingual situations, but one can also look upon this as a signature of diversity and in some ways cities like Bombay or Delhi have this feature of a polyglot situation.

To conclude, my basic argument is that cultures are plural, we should understand them as processes, and we should emphasize shared histories and oppose cultural essentialism. This means that cultures are not given entities; they should be seen as problems, as changing, not as fixed units. This is a counter balance to arguments for cultural specificity and uniqueness which are used as political weapons to establish a ground in order to fight somebody else. Seeing cultures as processes gives us an insight into the normalcy of pluricultural and multilingual contexts.

This does have implications for academic work as well. The normal way in which we communicate with each other is the dialogue and the dialogue – although it is epistemological not just between 'I and you' – is nevertheless bipolar. And it leads to the whole question of bilateralism in politics and the question of unequal power relations which make open dialogue impossible. Since I am arguing in favor of diversity, I am for a situation of multilateralism. So *Gespräche* or conversation is a good term. But one suggestion which some philosophers have made is to use the term 'polylog' and the term 'polylog' as opposed to the term 'dialog' works in terms of multiple networks of communication which are not only between 'you and me' but between 'us'. So it is a lateral way of communication and it is much closer to the notion of a 'tapestry of culture' or the whole notion of what you might call the network or the web of cultural relationships. The political task is then to work towards democratisation of the system of exchanges so that unequal power relations are overcome.

References

Amin, Samir: Capitalism in the Age of Globalization. The Management of Contemporary Society, London 1977

Bhatti, Anil: Diversität und Homogenisierung, in: Diskussionsforum: Postkoloniale Arbeiten/Postcolonial Studies; www.goethezeitportal.de/index.php?id=1431 [15. 10. 2010]

Chakrabarty, Dipesh: Provincializing Europe. Postcolonial Thought and Historical Difference, New Delhi 2001 [Princeton 2000]

Chatterjee, Partha (ed.): Wages of Freedom. Fifty Years of the Indian Nation-State, Delhi 1998

Conrad, Sebastian/Randeria, Shalini (eds.): Jenseits des Eurozentrismus. Postkoloniale Perspektiven in den Geschichts- und Kulturwissenschaften, Frankfurt am Main/New York 2002

Csáky, Moritz/Zeyringer, Klaus (eds.): Ambivalenz des kulturellen Erbes. Vielfachcodierung des historischen Gedächtnisses, Innsbruck 2000

Feichtinger, Johannes/Stachel, Peter: Das Gewebe der Kultur. Kulturwissenschaftliche Analysen zur Geschichte und Identität Österreichs in der Moderne, Innsbruck 2001

Herder, Johann Gottfried: Ideen zur Philosophie der Geschichte der Menschheit, ed. by Martin Bollacher, Frankfurt am Main 1989

Mozeti, Gerhard (ed.): Austromarxistische Positionen, Wien 1983

Musil, Robert: Tagebücher, Aphorismen, Essays und Reden, ed. by Adolf Frise, Hamburg 1955

Nehru, Jawaharlal: The Discovery of India, London 1946

Pannikar, K.N.: Culture, Ideology, Hegemony. Intellectuals and Social Consciousness in Colonial India, New Delhi 1995

Patnaik, Prabhat: The Retreat to Unfreedom. Essays on the Emerging World Order, New Delhi 2003

Tagore, Rabindranath: Nationalism, London 1917

Thapar, Romila: History and Beyond, New Delhi 2000

Turk, Horst/Schultze, Brigitte/Simanowski, Roberto (eds.): Kulturelle Grenzziehungen im Spiegel der Literaturen. Nationalismus, Regionalismus, Fundamentalismus, Göttingen 1998

Wimmer, Franz: Polylog der Traditionen im philosophischen Denken, in: *Ram Adhar Mall/ Notker Schneider* (eds.): Ethik und Politik aus interkultureller Sicht (= Studien zur interkulturellen Philosophie, No. 5), 1996, pp. 39-54

Wolf, Eric: Europe and the People Without History, Berkeley/Los Angeles 2000 [1982]

What Is Characteristic of Europe's Unity of Values?

Hans Lenk

According to the model constitution for Europe developed in 2003-2004 but not yet legally accepted, Europe is considered a "community of common values" and of a joint history – despite all the internal strife, tensions and pluralisms among European nations, differences that seem to have by now been overcome within the European Union, which was initially of economic provenance.

However, what is the specific and characteristic combination of these values? That is to say, what constitutes them beyond the international dissemination of those so-called Western values that have lately been debated worldwide under the topic of 'Human Rights' (whether universal or not) in concentrating, for example, on East-West or North-South differences as well as on varying interpretations of the UN Declaration of Human Rights of 1948.

In the proposed Constitution of Europe (2000), it is emphasised that a union would be "founded on the values of respect for human dignity, liberty, democracy, quality, the rule of law and respect for human rights, including the rights of persons belonging to minorities" (article I-2)[1], values that are common to the European member states. However, after the overwhelming acceptance worldwide of the UN Declaration of Human Rights, these values will certainly also be accepted on many other continents. Therefore, we cannot understand them as the only characteristic criteria of European values. Even if additional and more concrete norms and value orientations like "non-discrimination", "tolerance", "justice", "solidarity" and "equality between women and men" are added as well as a "pluralism" of cultural traditions and languages etc., this will not give rise to a specific characterising singularity of the European value system – especially if we consider that European values have had a decisive impact on the rest of the so-called Western world as well as on the concepts of human rights all over the world. Also, the idea that the Constitution has added "new values", "notably human dignity, equality, the rights of minorities and the characterization of the values upheld by the societies of the member states" does not deliver such a criterion of singularity. The same is true for the objectives of the European Union, including "freedom, security and justice without internal frontiers, and internal free market", "sustainable development based on balanced economic growth and price stability" and a "high level of protection and improvement of the quality of the environment." The refusing of social exclusion and discrimination and the promotion of social security and the protection of and "respect" for "cultural and linguistic diversity" and "cultural heritages" especially "Europe's

1 See e. g. http://europa.eu/scadplus/constitution/objectives_en.htm [15. 10. 2010].

cultural heritage" (article I-3). Also, the great 'four freedoms' – of persons, goods, services and capital – within the union and the strict prohibition of any discrimination on grounds of nationality or race, sex, etc. is not specific to Europe.

The preliminary European Constitution also includes the tradition of human rights as formulated not only in the Universal Declaration of Human Rights by the UN in 1948 but also in the European Convention for the Protection of Human Rights and Fundamental Freedoms (1950), in the form of the Charter of Fundamental Rights, which was solemnly established in the year 2000 on the occasion of the Nice European Council.

If we want to trace a more *specific* combination of the structure of European values and objectives, we have to go back to history and the descendents of some basic traditions, values and principles of Europe's fundamental cultural orientations, which certainly stem from a variety of historical and cultural roots.

First of all we have to look for a manifold combination of cultural ideas and influences derived from the philosophy of the Greeks, from the ideas of Christianity and Judaism as well as from the notions of rights and the culture of the law and jurisdiction that originated with Roman legal traditions. All these multicultural branches and influences have combined to develop a certain dynamic structure not only in theory, but particularly in the practical realms of life, e. g. in those economic relationships in the form of markets restrained and directed by laws, in the differentiation of political sovereignty and also in religious orientations, etc.

Studies on cultural values and their roots in Europe[2] usually mention freedom and liberty, appreciation of life on the social level, self-realization, the centrality of 'internalization' ('*Innerlichkeit*') as well as rationality and the acceptance of morality[3] – in addition to 'transcendence', i. e. the separation of the mundane and divine in the differentiation between religion and public life, or philosophy and the state, etc. The separation of the worldly or mundane realm from the divine or religious realm of spirituality would be a specific unity in connotation, prepared during the Middle Ages, but coming fully to the forefront in the periods of the Reformation and the Enlightenment. For instance, Christian Meier would thus see the development of culture from freedom instead of domination of power as the formula for the basic development of the Greek world, although liberty and freedom in ancient Greece in fact also depended on the works of slavery and were restricted to the free burghers. In the Christian religious tradition, freedom was transformed from an idea of the absence of restrictions into a valuable 'independence' as a positive objective. According to Patterson, Christianity would be the first and only world religion which would declare freedom to be a positive religious aim and objective

2 See e. g. *Joas, Hans/Wiegandt, Klaus* (eds.): Die kulturellen Werte Europas, Frankfurt am Main 2005.

3 Ibid., pp. 19.

(St. Paul's Epistle to the Galatians, Luther and Protestantism) leading towards a "culture of individual autonomy" (Charles Taylor) by interpreting the rights and self-development of any single human being – even when in tension with society – to the idea of an individualistic freedom in the private and public sphere, something that Peter Wagner[4] also underlines. Indeed, all of the following seem to be particularly characteristic of the European tradition all the way through to the present day: Greek philosophy's ideas of truth and reason, and the Stoic notions of humanitarianism or humanity according to Panaetius and later Cicero, and the notion of individualism (which is, I think, a very important contribution by Socrates), as well as the Christian valuation of the human life as an high asset of any human being *in concreto*.

Besides the birth of practical or concrete humanity (humanitarianism or the idea of humaneness) in the tradition of ancient Chinese philosophers such as Confucius and (above all) Mencius (who was the founder of what I call 'concrete' or practical humanity),[5] it is the combination of Greek and in particular Stoic philosophy of the humane human being as well as the Christian emphasis on the high(est) value of the human individual that are of the utmost importance for the history of values and culture. To be sure, the Greek idea of reason or rationality, their approach to argumentation and rational justifications, would also be a very important criterion.

The emphasis on individualism and freedom would certainly lead to the respect and tolerance of pluralistic traditions in terms of value orientations and virtues as well as morality. The ideas of non-discrimination, pluralism etc., equality of cultural traditions as well as the rights of different cultural groups including minorities would certainly derive therefrom.

In general, I think that the papers as well as the discussion thus far have not taken this combination of individualism and practical (concrete) humanity into enough consideration. Even the spread of the UN Declaration of Human Rights seems to be a bit abstract, i. e. too formal, to be able to delve more deeply into the problems of the concretisation of humanitarianism in the mentioned sense. Of course, the Declaration could only ever be such a rather moral and legal instrument of high generality.

Even those books on the cultural values of Europe, for example that of Joas/Wiegandt – colourful and differentiated as they are – do not, to my mind, sufficiently differentiate and develop this idea of a specific orientation towards individualism, humanitarianism and personal autonomy, though the idea of human dignity is of central importance everywhere in these works.

4 *Wagner, Peter*: Hat Europa eine kulturelle Identität? in: *Hans Joas/Klaus Wiegandt* (eds.): Die kulturellen Werte Europas, Frankfurt am Main 2005, p. 502.

5 See *Hans Lenk*: Konkrete Humanität, Frankfurt am Main 1998.

Socratic and Christian individualism and humanitarianism as well as Stoic humanism come together. It is not by chance that the humanistic orientation of the middle Stoics and especially Cicero cultivated not only humanism and humanitarianism as practised in every day life (think of Cicero's *homo humanus*) but also the idea of human dignity (*dignitas humana*), which dates back to Cicero before being rediscovered later on by the Renaissance[6] and by Herder (who is still today a somewhat underrated philosopher of concrete humanity and humanitarianism[7]).

The specific orientation of the concrete human being resulted not only in the Christian 'love thy neighbour' as well as the remotest human being whatsoever, but also in the form of humanitarian practitioners and philosophers like Albert Schweitzer and Mother Theresa in a particular programme of humanitarianism which certainly does not apply only to Europe but can also be found in different Indian traditions (for example, in the figure of Gandhi), although these latter ones are mostly not clad in the form of an activist approach to the world, but are more passive like the *ahimsa*-norm of Indian ethics.

Specifically, Europeans seem to be endowed with the combination of this kind of practical humanitarianism and care for the other *in active terms* with the idea of solidarity – one of the three leading ideas of the French Revolution, next to freedom and equality.

It seems to be characteristically continental European that this kind of solidarity has even survived and invaded the economic world and that we have not only liberal markets of nearly unfettered capitalism nowadays, but also what is called a 'social market economy' ('*soziale Marktwirtschaft*'). The latter does not appear to have been exported together with the economic orientation in general – at least not as successfully as it is still held up in the continent of 'old' Europe.

It is true that there seems as yet not to be a 'European identity' in the narrower sense defined by abstract or universal values, but instead an idea of European identity as an ideal or normative concept that appears to concentrate on shared values, values which have to be interpreted and experienced however, if not engendered in some sense. We have no cultural property *per se*[8] – this has to be interpreted on grounds of a certain kind of common historical experience. That is, the idea of Europe has somehow to be installed or set up as a value in the first place. As a specific value, this idea of Europe is certainly an ideal construct to be fulfilled and properly materialised in the future; it has certainly a normative plea, just as the fundamental

6 E. g. *Pico della Mirandola, Giovanni*: De Hominis Dignitate. Über die Würde des Menschen, ed. by August Buck, Hamburg 1990 [1496].

7 See *Lenk*, 1998, and *Lenk, Hans*: Humanité effective et éducation à la tolerance. Droits de l'homme positifs, créativité et eigen-activité, in: UNESCO (ed.): La philosophie et la protection des droits humains, Paris 2006, pp. 45-70.

8 *Wagner*, 2005, pp. 497.

principles and values in the extant model constitution of Europe do. Thus, the building of Europe and its values is an ongoing and at times difficult task. This is true regarding the different traditions, languages and nationalities in this old continent.

However, one may well ask[9] whether the traditional religious wars, the Reformation and the tensions between European cultural traditions as mentioned above would have opened up the question and led to a respectful plurality of human life. It seems quasi natural that the ideas of tolerance and non-discrimination would be especially emphasised in and by European institutions – I'm thinking here of rational argumentation, value comparison, cultural and multicultural relationships as well as the respective formal law of intercultural international relations (see, e. g., the tradition of International Law). Even the UN Declaration of Human Rights is an outcome of this, although in its intended universalism it restricts itself to mainly Western values and cultural traditions, and not to various Eastern values or group/tribal values, etc. The extension of historical origin and the roots of an idea like that of an intercultural and universal value system would only be possible by transcending the actual historical origin and its development. Thus, the UN Declaration has to be understood in such a universal human sense in general not as a rather *European* enterprise of transporting Western values, norms, objectives, etc. This is particularly true with respect to the old idea of moral human rights in ancient China – '*ren*' by Confucius and his followers –, and especially regarding practical (concrete) humanity as worked out, defended and strongly emphasised by Mencius, and which amounts to a full-fledged humanitarianism regarding contextual and situational applications for all walks of practical life.

Thus, we can follow Peter Wagner[10] in his assessment that in answering the question relating to the European cultural identity he would be uttering a 'cautious yes'. As an idea, this identity can only gain validity by orienting actions and judgements as well as their respective representing groups not in the form of a territorial, political or cultural unity alone, but as an open, pluralistic, multi- and intercultural conglomerate of orientations based on the UN Declaration of Human Rights as well as some specific traits of the mentioned European interpretation of value orientations like freedom and liberty, solidarity, the idea of equality, individual autonomy, human dignity, individualism and, as I think, most importantly, concrete humanity or humanitarianism – even with respect to certain non-human creatures and ecosystems as nature.

An extended idea of such a humanitarian orientation was, after Herder (1792-94), developed in the last century by the famous 'jungle doctor' and philosopher of culture, Albert Schweitzer, who to my mind is one of the outstanding paragons of an *homo europeus* in the true sense, combining theoretical reflection, argumentation,

9 Ibid., p. 504.
10 Ibid., p. 510.

philosophy and ethics with an activist approach toward all walks of life, as well as Christian love (*caritas*) and devoted practical engagement. Albert Schweitzer was a living example for that characteristically European combination of values that I have been talking about. As an Alsatian, having lived, worked and studied in Strasbourg and also having worked on another continent on humanitarian projects under the leading idea of '*caritas*' (charity), he is indeed one of the outstanding paragons of an ideal European displaying the best of European values and humanitarianism.

References

Herder, Johann Gottfried: Briefe zur Beförderung der Humanität, in: *ibid.*: Werke in zwei Bänden, ed. by Karl-Gustav Gerold, Vol. 2, München 1953, pp. 458-671

Joas, Hans/Wiegandt, Klaus (eds.): Die kulturellen Werte Europas, Frankfurt am Main 2005

Lenk, Hans: Konkrete Humanität, Frankfurt am Main 1998

Lenk, Hans: Humanité effective et éducation à la tolerance. Droits de l'homme positifs, créativité et eigen-activité, in: UNESCO (ed.): La philosophie et la protection des droits humains, Paris 2006, pp. 45-70

Pico della Mirandola, Giovanni: De Hominis Dignitate. Über die Würde des Menschen, ed. by August Buck, Hamburg 1990 [1496]

Schweitzer, Albert: Die Lehre von der Ehrfurcht vor dem Leben, München 1962

Schweitzer, Albert: Kultur und Ethik, München 1923

Schweitzer, Albert: Über Humanität, in: *ibid.*: Wie wir überleben, Freiburg/Basel/Wien 1994

http://europa.eu/scadplus/constitution/objectives_en.htm [15. 10. 2010]

Culture Fortress Europa.
On the Necessity and Impossibility of Being European

J. Peter Burgess

Insider-Outsider in Europe

When I first moved to Norway 18 years ago, I had already lived and studied in Europe for many years. So I was already involved in the inside-outside dance of Europe and its others. That changed when, innocently reading European philosophy at the *Staatsbibliothek* in Berlin in 1989, I met my future wife, a charming design student from western Norway.

Of course, I was, according to a certain definition, already then an *outsider* in Berlin and in Europe. When I moved to Oslo one year later, I was again, though in an entirely different way and according to an entirely different logic, an *outsider* in Norway and Europe. Still, the complexity did not stop there. I was quickly to learn that the imbrication of inside and outside was doubled and redoubled through marriage, offspring, employment, education, location, language, space and time.

Thus, on the one hand, I became *more* European by marrying and starting a family with a European. Along that particular axis I became an *insider*. But I quickly understood that this was only *one kind* of insider, itself imbedded in a new outsiderness. I became a member of the outsider-insider group, that special class of Norwegians who are essentially outsiders recognised and to some degree integrated inside Norwegian society. *Insider* to a family, but always culturally (and genealogically) *outside*, installing myself in a cosmopolitan city as part of a kind of international mobile elite, *included* in the circles of foreigners (French was my working language at the time, and I began my career at the Lycée Français of Oslo), yet *excluded* from the traditional Norwegian intellectual circles. At the same time I was, and still am seen as *more European* than most Norwegians, even the educated. From my education to the languages I speak, to the way I dress, to the food I eat and to my decadent insistence on enjoying a glass of wine at dinner.

On the other hand, as you are aware, Norway itself also has a strange *outsider* status in Europe. It is formally not a member of the European Union, but follows the EU laws and directives far more strictly and conscientiously than most Member States. The urban political elite in Norway consider themselves entirely European, while the rural majority for the most considers Norway a thing apart.

Innflyter

This constellation of logics of *belonging* was further complicated itself when I moved with wife and newborn daughter from Oslo to my wife's village on the west coast of Norway in 1993. Driven in part by my own wildly naïve rural romanticism (of a kind only an urban outsider can possess), we set up housekeeping on an old farm that had belonged to my wife's family for generations. Here I became, in an entirely new way, an *outsider* again. Yet I still had not understood the degree to which I was an outsider.

One day a minor dispute about car-parking on our property line revealed to me dimensions of my outsider-ness of which I was hardly aware. In the heat of the argument our new neighbours called me an *innflyter*. This I interpreted as a kind of simple nationalism, pitting in immigrant against national natives. But this was far too simple. For it was not simply because I was a 'foreigner' who had moved to Norway from abroad several years before, spoke Norwegian with a foreign accent, etc. (though this was certainly one part of it). Nor was I an *innflyter* because I was a non-European who had moved to Europe. It was not even because I had moved from Norway's capital to the rural region where I had no traditional ties. No, I was an *innflyter* because I was part of a family that lived in the village and had moved out to the farm!

The Idea of Europe

The overlapping rings of inclusion and exclusion, of ownership and belonging, of titles and rights, of obligation and privileges before those who are unlike us is deeply complex. They present just as much a challenge to our hearts and minds as they present a challenge to our political institutions. Europe is only one example of a cultural identity, seemingly self-evident and at the same time deeply at odds with itself. What is a 'European' anyway?

The *idea* of Europe long outdates the existence of Europe. It will doubtless outlive it. All institutional projects involve ideas, of course. But few political projects have known such a rich and long-standing intellectual or imaginary basis. It is possible to reconstruct a genealogy of Europe as far back as early Greek thought. It is a certain set of values arising out of the meeting of Greek and Latin culture, a constellation of notions about the rights and obligations of human beings that emerged from the Renaissance, a certain number of politico-moral principles serving as the motor for the American and French Revolutions. In short, the intellectual and spiritual legacy of Europe is deeply rooted in two millennia of history of a continent in search of its spiritual identity. On the other side of the coin, the consequences of the Industrial Revolution, first in the 18th century in the United Kingdom, then in the early 19th century on the European continent sharpened the sense that Europe was also a material reality. Thus Saint-Simon, on the eve of Versailles, and thirty years before the publication of the Communist Manifesto, wrote an impassioned plea for a European Parliament based on a conception of a Europe united by *material* conditions, as an arena in which mass industrialisation opposes a new collective working class to a new kind of reality, itself opened by a new sense of internationalism.

The 2nd century B.C. Hellenistic poet Moschos of Syracuse tells the well-known story of the abduction of Europe. The Phoenician maiden Europa frolics on the beaches of Lebanon. The god Zeus sees her and becomes infatuated. He transforms himself into a bull and approaches her. She becomes fascinated, climbs on his back. Zeus carries her westward across the water to Crete where they mate and form the European race. Much has been said about this myth. (Most strikingly it describes the birth of Europe in turns of an abduction and rape.) But perhaps more important for the question of who Europeans are is this story's status as *myth*. Europe is a myth, a *necessary* myth, one whose origin is far beyond gaze, but the power of whose mystery carries on.

Immigration in the EU

The present debate on European migration, asylum and visa policies has its origin in the Treaty of the European Union, signed at Maastricht in 1992. The treaty, which marked the transition from the European Commission to the European Union, significantly expanded the competence of the Union to carry out actions. The treaty both created the *euro* and set up the three *pillars* of current EU institutional architecture. In particular, the Justice and Home Affairs pillar brought migration to the forefront of politics and public attention.

The population of the European Union lies at around 493 million people. Of these, 18.5 million (or about 3.8 %) are third-country nationals. The most important groups of third-country nationals are citizens of Turkey, Morocco, Albania and Algeria. Most new residents of the EU settle in Greece, Italy, Spain and the U.K. Since 2002 net immigration has oscillated between 1.5 and 2 million people per year.

There are also important demographic and economic issues involved: Recent projections suggest that there will be a natural decrease in the EU population between 2010 and 2050. Assuming zero net immigration, the population of the EU would be about 26 million people less in 2030 than it is today, and 50 million less in 2050.

In economic terms, the main change will involve the size of the working-age population, which, to follow current trends, will decrease by 69 million by 2050. The EU will go from having four to only two people of working-age for each citizen aged 65 and above.[1]

Thus the question of third-country nationals is constantly on today's political agenda and increasingly intertwined with the question of the security of Europeans, both *internal* and *external*. Who *is* and *is not* a European is profoundly tied to who or what *threatens* Europeans.

The question of migration is of course very complex, and has among others cultural, social, political, economic and religious dimensions. What distinguishes it in particular, however, is that it *re-opens sub-European issues*. Clearly, migration has immediate consequences for those people who have the most direct contact with migrants. National and sub-national institutions, regional cultures and local societies have the most concrete contact the influx of foreign cultures. Thus the paradox that structures European cultural identity: At the very moment when Europe formulates a general approach to third-country nationals, based on common principles and universal ideas, the national and sub-national issues return with a vengeance. Our experience of *European-ness*, of *Europe under threat* emphasises our place in local spheres of experience.

European Identity?

Thus, more than ever before, the question of *European identity* becomes an acutely political one. Not only is the question *who we are* more central than ever, but also *who decides who we are,* and the slightly more scientific question, *on what grounds, according to what criterion are we who we are*? The need for answers to these questions seems acute in our time. Consequently *European-ness*, *European identity* and *the European* are now invested with enormous power and potential. It is almost as though a certain European pathology produces the need for the concept of the European, itself driven on by a need to concretise it.

From a certain point of view the concept of European identity functions as a collective attempt to convince ourselves that European-ness really exists, and to re-assure ourselves that we indeed belong to it. In the last two centuries of European history, this *conceptual pathology* has corresponded to a kind of inflation of the scope of the concept of 'the European' in the form of European civilisation. Thus the *mission cilvilisatrice* of the 19th century played itself out through the great self-proclaimed 'Europe Builders', from Alexander to Genghis Kahn, to Charlemagne, to Caesar, to

1 *Commission of the European Communities*: Communication from the Commission to the European Parliament, the Council, the European Economic and Social Committee and the Committee of the Regions towards a Common Immigration Policy; http://www.libertysecurity.org/IMG/pdf_com 2007_0780en01.pdf [02. 12. 2009].

Hitler, they all fought for an ever-expanding geopolitical Europe and a contentious concept of Europe. This drive has to a large degree burnt out in the 21st century. The expansionist, civilisation phase of European history is clearly over. The European, once an outward looking mode, has long become and *inward looking, defensive* mode.

Identity is Hybrid

This is linked to the nature of a global reality in which the flow of cultural influences moves in all directions and carries many different types of meaning. European identity is more than ever before *hybrid.* It has many axes and many orientations. Though in conflict on one level, they are harmonious on another. Indeed, it is by means of the conflictual nature of identities – the productive inner conflicts – that one comes to know oneself. This, as we will see, is the key to the insider-outsider relation of European identity.

Identity, be it European or otherwise, bursts its own categories just as it constitutes them. What is 'the European' today? Is it the fact that one carries a European passport? Is the fact that one speaks a European language? Or that one was born in a European country or has a European partner? No, for the European is infinitely more complex, rich and ambivalent. Indeed if Europeans *are* something, if Europeans have *one* certain identity at any *one* given time, it is most unambiguously the quality of being indeterminate.

At the same time, it is important to underscore that it is not us who decide. This logic of identity, the production and evolution of cultural identity, does not *belong* to us. The mechanisms and structures that form our identity are not part of us; they are already part of an other, an outsider. We are never authors of our own identity, no matter how often we think we are. Efforts to consolidate European identity, programmes such as the European Cities of Culture, the Year of Culture, etc. have effects on identity, but they are strangely and – wonderfully – unpredictable.

In this sense, whenever we might attempt to determine, by formal or informal means, who is a European, that very question is unavoidably preceded by another question, namely, who should decide who is a European. A European? Someone else? And when we pose the question to that person, on what grounds can we know that s/he is right? By what authority is the claim made? Who is the other? Do we know ourselves adequately enough to say who we are and who future insiders shall be?

Internal and External Identity

Externally, one's identity is formed in opposition to other identities, to neighbours or friends, to other groups or collectives. It can also clearly be formed through opposition to enemies. All of the *external* sources of identity represent, at one level or another, *threats* to one's identity. They represent, in benevolent cases, the persistence of knowledge or consciousness of *who or what we are not*. In malevolent cases they actually represent threats to one's existence.

Internally, one's identity is deeply involved in a relationship to oneself, to a self-perception, to one's self-understanding. The sense of self at the heart of the individual, at the heart of the European, for example, is dependent upon the gaze of the other, dependent upon the recognition of the other. In order to be oneself, a person is doubled. I am who I am, and yet my sense of that self is bound up in the regard of others, and upon my regard of the regard of others.

One might think that I am painting a dreadful picture, somewhere between crisis and schizophrenia. The centre of my message is that identity can never be taken as a sure thing in debates about who we are, what our identity is, European or otherwise, and what that alleged identity entitles us to.

Identity always takes the form of identity politics, of a negotiation, a *negotiation* for what we are, a debate whose terms we cannot write ourselves. In other words: yes, we must talk about identity. But if we are authentically and openly talking about it, then we know and recognise that the beginning and end of that debate are out of our hands. If we think we are in control of the terms of reference of the debate when we possess the power of definition and pass judgements on the legitimacy, then we know that, though we may be talking about many things, we are not talking about identity.

Responsibility: Impossibility and Necessity

I close with a word about responsibility. As in any culture, Europeans are *insiders* outside and *outsiders* inside, strangers to themselves. European cultural identity is never entirely present. Even in its most concrete formulations in the legal documents of integration and citizenship it is a condensation of memories of the past and aspirations for the future, ultimately impossible to bind. We can never know it entirely and yet we always have a need to know, in order to choose our path, our ethics, etc. This is the experience of cultural identity. We are constantly moving toward a future that is unknown to us. The European future will take a form that is unknown to us and yet toward which we must – today – plot a course.

The alternatives seem hopeless. Responsibility to our future implies *necessarily* responding in an *impossible* way, based on impossible knowledge. We must invent our path, our future without entirely knowing who we are and where we are going, without entirely knowing who belongs and who does not, without being able to decide who is an insider and who is an outsider.

Knowledge, experience, logic and insight are all necessary and yet they fall short. And yet they *must* fall short. We are after all not machines. The humanity of cultural identity is precisely this pathos: it is absolutely indispensable, and yet we cannot know it absolutely. It is the experience of necessity and impossibility.

Islam in Europe/Europe Against Islam! Europe, Open Your Eyes

Nasr H. Abu Zaid †

Ladies and Gentlemen,

I would like to thank the organisers of this remarkable event for giving me the honour of presenting the keynote speech of this conference. It is a great honour with a heavy responsibility as well. I did not change the initial title of my proposed lecture, 'Europe, Open Your Eyes'. Instead, I made it the subtitle because I think it is still very much in line with this presentation, 'Islam in Europe/Europe against Islam!'. The demand for Europe to open her eyes implies both the literal and the figurative meanings; the physical meaning is intended, because Europeans are no longer a white skin race at odds with the yellow, black or colored skins of other nations. The figurative meaning is meant to show the deep historical contact between Europe and/or the West on the one hand and the Muslim World on the other hand. The exclamation point in the title could be replaced by a question mark as well, because this relation is definitely a problematic issue that needs a thorough investigation and a responsible, careful treatment.

Islam is Part of Europe

The present situation, especially the 'war on terror' campaign waged by the USA which led to the empowerment of the terrorist's ideology of *us* against *them*, seems to be discouraging. In fact, it is. Nevertheless, giving up is a suicide-decision we need to avoid. We need to dig deep in our shared human history to uncover the cultural roots of our humanity. The modern, advanced and powerful West, whatever the concept West designates, has to discover that its scientific and technological progress was only possible because it was built on what other earlier civilisations, including the civilisation of the Muslims, achieved. Muslims, on the other hand, need to recognise the historical fact that the Arabs, the original carriers of the Islamic message into the world, could not have achieved the building of the great civilisation of Islam on their own. It was possible due to the multi-cultural, multi-ethnic and multi-religious composition of the Umayyad and the Abbasid Empires, not to mention the Fatimid dynasty in the East and the Andalusian dynasty in the West, in Spain. This composition enhanced the development of the philosophical, theological, mystical, legal and cultural openness that characterises the Muslim civilisation. More important for both the West and the Muslim world is the recognition of the fact that the distinction between them is entirely artificial. Islam has become part of the West, just as the West is present everywhere in the world of Islam. Europe, in particular, has to reorient itself to the colourful composition of its citizens; white is no longer the only European skin colour. Europe also needs to redefine its identity to embrace Islam not necessarily as a religion, but as an essential component of its cultural identity which is currently under reconstruction.This is historical fact. The 20th century witnessed a great movement of migration for different reasons, and Muslims have now become part of the European demography.

Counterproductive Discourse

The immediate reaction to September 11th everywhere has put the West/Europe at odds with Islam. An atmosphere of mistrust of the Muslims emerged in the West; every Muslim became a suspect, which generated a feeling of insecurity and mistrust among Muslims themselves. In its invasion of Afghanistan and the occupation of Iraq, the 'war on terror' has already been a great failure; terrorism has became more widespread and al-Qaeda's leadership is out of reach. London and Madrid suffered, as well as Indonesia, Morocco and Egypt.

The murder of Van Gogh in the Netherlands in November 2004 caused real shock for Muslims as well as for non-Muslims. The immediate reaction was extremely irrational; every Muslim became a criminal and Islam became a defendant. Things have started to calm down now and there is serious discussion and intellectual debate about the future. Nevertheless, there are some radical Dutch politicians and some radical neo-liberal and fundamentalist rational intellectuals who keep propagating anti-Islamic discourse. Those intellectuals – and there are others all over Europe and the USA – identify Islam as an essentially jihadist violent doctrine directed mainly against the West; they claim Islam is a dangerous religion which is going to destroy the West ant demolish Western culture. They attack the Koran, and some would like to have the book legally banned; a film expressing this message is about to be released. It will be another episode of using art to defame Islam after the earlier film 'Submission', written be Ian Hersi Ali and directed by Van Gogh in 2004, and after the Danish cartoon controversy in 2005. I think this kind of political as well as intellectual discourse against Islam is counterproductive and irresponsible. Since Islam is now a part of Europe and Muslims are a part of the European demography, defaming Islam is – or should be considered – a defamation of Europe. This is, in my view, one of the essential reasons behind the failure of integration.

Muslims are not immigrants anymore; they are born, brought up and educated in European schools. Some young Muslim citizens (generalisation is very dangerous here), second and third generation, and all across Europe, seem to suffer a feeling of not belonging; they don't belong to the European society, neither do they belong to the original countries of their parents or grandparents. With regards to language they are Europeans, but with regards to culture they are Muslims. Are they torn between these identities? Before I suggest any answer to this, allow me to quote an e-mail message I received some time ago. It is one example among hundreds of messages, but this one is from a German-Egyptian Muslim young man, and illustrates a certain identity problem: If somebody in Germany asks me where I am from I tell them that I am Egyptian. When I am in Egypt they immediately know that I was not born in Egypt. So actually I am neither Egyptian nor German. I think I came to terms with the fact that I am a traveler in between the two worlds which surely also impacts my spiritual life. Deep down inside of me there is a huge trust and confidence in God; it is a small light. This light makes me seek for truth regarding Islam. But to find truth is not that easy, especially when you are not a scholar.

When I look into the Koran, which I can only read in German or English, as I have never learnt Arabic, there are things that make me wonder and things that I simply do not understand or that I am not able to make sense of. So searching for wisdom is not that easy compared to somebody who is a scholar. I have to follow my instinct a bit more and hope that there are some scholars out there who deliver some facts or inspire me. Despite the fact that I have not read very much about mainstream Islamic theology, deep down inside of me I strongly feel that there must be another way; otherwise, I will have a big problem in making sense of the current interpretation/theology of Islam. It is funny that I say that because when I talk to my 'Western' friends, I would always reply that they cannot judge Islam by evaluating current Islamic society.

As long as we keep on moving as human beings new things will open up. So I kept on moving and I came across you. It was a great experience getting to know some of your thoughts. I am still at the beginning, I have to say, but I am excited to read more about you. At the same time I know that I should also be reading mainstream thought and the replies to your thoughts provided that these people who are answering you have pure motives. The reason I am writing is that I simply wanted you to know that I am inspired by your thoughts and that you make a difference to the Islamic world.

Another voice, from France, is to be quoted as well: Abdelaziz Eljaouhari is the son of Berber Moroccan immigrants and an eloquent Muslim political activist. He talked with fluent passion, in perfect French, about the misery of the impoverished housing projects around Paris – which were again wracked by protests – and the chronic social discrimination against immigrants and their descendants. France's so-called 'Republican model', he said furiously, means in practice: "I speak French, am called Jean-Daniel and have blue eyes and blond hair." If you are called Abdelaziz, have darker skin and are Muslim, the French Republic does not practice what it preaches. "What *égalité* is there for us?" he asked. "What *liberté*? What *fraternité*?" And then he delivered his personal message to Nicolas Sarkozy, the French president, in words that I will never forget. "*Moi*," said Abdelaziz Eljaouhari, in a ringing voice, "*moi, je suis la France*!"

And, he might have added, *l'Europe*, for the profound alienation of many Muslims – especially the second and third generations of immigrant families, young men and women themselves born in Europe. If things continue to go as badly as they are at the moment, this alienation, and the way it both feeds and is fed by the resentment of mainly white, Christian or post-Christian Europeans, could tear apart the civic fabric of Europe's most established democracies.

Those young Muslims present an example. One is trying to identify his spiritual identity by looking into a way out of the dominant Islamic discourse; he is conducting his own search. The question is: How can we help people like him? The second is angry about assault and discrimination; he does not seem to have a problem of identity or a problem of integration. Nevertheless, he feels like an 'unwanted stranger' and also experiences a lack of 'equality'.

But do we not also have to be aware of those who suffer more serious identity crises, which makes it possible for them to identify with the ideology of anger and destruction, i. e. terrorism? These are serious questions that only psychoanalysts can tackle.

Non-Monolithic, Hyphenated Identities

What is the identity of an immigrant? Via the consideration of skin color and physical features, the person identified is as black African, white, Latin American, Asian, Arab, Indian or Japanese. If religion is considered, he or she would be identified as Christian, Jewish, Muslim, Buddhist or atheist. So identity is not built on one essential factor; it has so many facets in its structure. But the problem in the history of Europe was, and still is, that immigrants are identified according to one single dimension of their complex identity. Before World War II, the Jewish people were only identified as Jewish, not as German Jewish, French Jewish, or Dutch Jewish. In the Netherlands, where I live now and have been living for the last thirteen years, people who belong to different national backgrounds – Turks, Moroccans, Iraqis, Surinamese, etc. – are all identified only as Muslims. This tendency to identify people according to their religion has increased since September 11th, especially for those with a Muslim background. It does not make any difference whether those people are devout Muslims or not. Muslims, whether in Europe or in the USA, are not a hegemonic group. We should be careful about generalisations. They are ethnically and culturally different, whether we speak about Muslims from the Indian subcontinent, from Southeast Asia, from the Middle East or from Africa, not to mention European and American Muslim converts. Unfortunately, people tend to speak about Islam and about Muslims in a very naive and simplistic way, with no variations and no reference to history.

Within the EU establishment, the discussion about European identity has not yet reached a conclusion, as can be seen from the debate about the European Constitution. In the polemic discourse about Islam, there is always the claim of European culture, European values, etc. as being opposed to Islam. But what kind of Islam is Europe opposing? Here we can easily recognise the identification of Islam with all negative non-European values. The challenging question is how to deconstruct these monolithic concepts in order to show the diversity of cultures within both Europe and Islam. How many languages does Europe speak and how much is the budget for translation within the EU? How different are the British or French cultures from the German or Dutch cultures? Europe seems to be well identified only in comparison with Muslims and in the face of Islam; but how much of Europe's identity is actually a reaction against its own history and some of its own citizens?

Combating Fundamentalism

Dealing with the problem as a problem with Islam leads to the theologising of all issues involved; beyond that, it implicitly encourages the claim of radical Muslims that all the problems can easily be solved if people return to the true faith. Europe must remember that according to its modern values of Human Rights it granted refugee status and political asylum in the seventies and the eighties to so many advocates of radical Islam for humanitarian reasons – these were people being persecuted in their home countries. In fact, these protective humanitarian measures started as early as the fifties when some members of the Egyptian Muslim Brothers Association were persecuted. Without undermining the values which provided protection for such individuals, they were able to establish the mosques from which they propagated their radical Islam which, in the long run, influenced the second and the third generations of immigrant Muslims. There is no time or space here to deal with the complicated socio-political context which made this possible.

However, Europe must deal with fundamentalism politically, culturally and intellectually – and not reduce it to a security problem. Religion is not a temporal phenomenon; it is not a heat wave or a disease as some neo-liberals claim. Religion is a very serious matter; for its followers, it has to do with nothing less than the meaning of life.

We have to understand the rhetoric of the fundamentalist discourse in order to be able to combat it intellectually. Quoting Qur'anic verses and prophetic sayings out of context – and thus implying meanings that appeal to the populace's sentiment – is the major rhetorical tactic employed in fundamentalist discourse. A second tactic is found in the use of slogans that can easily be memorised and repeated, such as 'Islam is the solution', 'Islam is a religion and a state', 'the headscarf is female honour', 'death to the enemy of Allah', etc. Third, there is the stereotyping of historical figures and historical events and the glorification of the past as the golden era of Islam, an era that could and should be recovered by simply reviving the imagined faith and practice of the revered ancestors. The last rhetorical tactic is the condemnation of any dissenting viewpoints by labeling them heresy or apostasy.

Combating fundamentalism by employing similar rhetoric would strengthen its logic, and thus reproduce it. The rhetoric employed by radical liberal and/or radical rational European writers against fundamentalism does, in fact, validate its logic, and it does so by itself employing rhetorical slogans – such as our culture, our civilisation and our democracy –, slogans which imply the incompatibility of Islam and these values. This is the same claim propagated by the fundamentalist discourse.

Combating fundamentalism in Europe is not possible without realising the importance of dealing with the original intellectual resources of their discourse, which is the fundamentalist discourse in the Arab and the Muslim world. Freedom is the keyword in combating fundamentalism and terrorism whether in society at large or in the educational institutions in specific. As long as the governments of the Arab and the Muslim World control all the economic, political and cultural resources, corruption will always flourish. Only freedom can fight against this absolute darkness. Only freedom can lead to a de-radicalisation of the fundamentalist discourse. This is very possible when freedom is for all, including the islamists. Freedom will lay bare the meaningless of their rhetoric; they have to talk politics instead of manipulating the meaning of religion. We have to make use of all means available: teaching, writing and public debate via public lectures, the printed press, radio and TV interviews, etc.

My major concern, as a scholar, is to show the historical fact of acculturation, meaning that there is no such thing as an autonomous and independent culture; every culture has to give and take in order to stay alive. Islam and the West are just imagined concepts, whereas in the course of history they have invaded each other and also integrated within each other even while fighting the other. I always take myself as an example of a constructed identity. Egyptian Arab Muslim means that I carry in my blood multiple cultural components, Pharaonic, Greek, Roman, and Coptic as well as Arabic and Islamic. I studied and taught in the USA and in Japan and now I am in Europe. Who am I? Am I an Egyptian, an Arab, a Muslim or a European immigrant? I am all of these and should not reduce my identity to only one of them.

To conclude, there is a need to deconstruct the simple one-dimensional notion of identity, such as European and Muslim, in favor of complex multi-dimensional identities. Second, rethinking the concept of boundaries – whether cultural, ethnic or religious – should be a priority. The utopian concept of 'European Islam' propagated by some well-intentioned intellectuals seems to be at odds with the global world in which we live. This does not mean that there is only one single Islam, a claim which is historically incorrect; Islam has been coloured, and will continue to be coloured, by the diversity of cultures in which Muslims live. But to formulate a specific European version would raise the question: what is Europe after all? But before all of these considerations, and perhaps above all of them, we need to de-theologise the discussion; for the theologising of socio-political problems is the very definition of fundamentalism.

Being a Muslim Minority Today and the 'Spaces of Hope'

Tahir Abbas

I would like to start by saying a tremendous thank you to the organisers here in Germany for the invitation to be here today and to you, the audience, for taking such an interest. I have been asked to speak on the issue of being a Muslim minority in Britain. If spaces and spatiality are crucial for effective social interaction between different individuals and groups, then, arguably, in relation to Muslims in the current climate, we certainly have problems. So what are these problems? How are we to determine the solutions adequately and in a sustained way? In essence, some of the problems and solutions are quite entrenched in the workings of majority society as whole, and we must go back through the centuries to determine the nature of its origins.

The impact of three centuries of the Crusades nearly a thousand years ago, to the role of colonialism, particularly in India, but also in Africa and the Middle East over the last five hundred years are crucially significant. But it is post-war immigration, settlement, and adaptation that are of special interest – as Muslims in Britain are inheriting past societal indiscretions in relation to the Islamic world, many of which are on-going –, as is the negative impact this has for groups today, often arriving with little social, cultural and economic capital, but a great deal of motivation, courage and ambition.[1]

I believe that the solutions to many of the problems facing Muslims in Britain are not about pulling at culture or stretching the notions of values; rather, they are about economic opportunity coupled with equality of outcome. Some would argue that the problems facing Muslims across the globe are a result of centuries of inner theological decay, followed by rampant exploitation by the colonisers, and the subsequent inheritance of post-colonial democratic systems of governance that have never really had a chance to get out of the starting blocks. But as argued by the greatest social historian ever known to man (and woman) today, Ibn Khaldun (1332-1406), all empires rise and fall, and we are seeing it before our eyes. The Ghosts of Empire are still in the machine of English society. How can they not be? After all, it has only been 60 years since its end, and at its height it reigned supreme. Not bad for what started off as bunch of pirates off the Caribbean seas.

Britain is still grappling with its demise as a world power. Meanwhile, Muslims in Muslim lands have no space to develop local, regional and national infrastructures. In the heartland of the Muslims, education is suppressed or channelled in particularly negative ways so as to deliberately prevent the masses from challenging the

1 *Abbas, Tahir*: British Islam. The Road to Radicalism, Cambridge 2009.

hegemon – particularly in the case of Saudi Arabia, where the wealth of twenty percent of the world's oil reserves rests in the hands of around 5,000 members of a royal family. No major western democracies make a commotion about that, leading to arguments of double-standards in the Muslim world.

In Western Europe, where there are approximately 20 million Muslims, they are often from the poorest parts of the sending countries – whether it is Anatolian Turks or the Azad Kashmiris; both groups respectively came to work in German and British motor and vehicle manufacturing industries in the early 1960s.[2] In relation to France, according to my good friend and colleague, Professor François Burgat, if you want to think of Muslims in France, think of one word: *Algeria*. And, when these jobs disappeared, their deskilling and under-employment led to unemployment or self-employment in the most marginal of economic sectors. As a result, the groups are effectively trapped in the very same areas they originally came to. And now we come back to economics and space.

Back in Britain, during the 1980s – much was made of identities. In the late 1980s, Norman Tebbit gave sports fans of my generation much to think about. Where does your loyalty lie when it comes to Cricket, he asked? Do you support Pakistan or England? Well that was easy, Pakistan. Because it was *and* probably is the only thing Pakistan is good at (I say with a touch of sarcasm). It felt good that the once colonial master got the occasional whopping by all the brown-skins, including what became India and the West Indies... and then Sri Lanka and Bangladesh...

Today, in asking me who I support when it comes to cricket, I would say, yes, reclaiming the Ashes in 2005 was a great achievement, and it was done, in part, with the aid of a Muslim and a Sikh bowling pair. The reason I supported England less during the 1980s was that apart from being pretty useless, it was because the selectors tended to exclude African-Caribbean and South Asians. But, when England drops its non-white players today, and we lose, it begins to pain me. The Rushdie Affair of 1989 illustrated how little people really knew or cared about Muslims, and how majority society is obsessed with its quaint ethnocentrisms, and with its once vainglorious positions as arbiters of global wealth. Of course, this event also illustrated how out of touch Muslims are with secular liberal democracies, where freedom of speech is considered a building block of modern societies.[3]

In the current period, we know from sociological research on labour markets that there is an 'ethnic penalty' for specific ethnic minorities, but in more recent periods the question of whether there is a further 'Muslim penalty' is also of special interest. In relation to housing, the problems of today's residential clustering, (not segregation, which can be a politically loaded concept), are a function of past failures of

2 West Europe's Muslims and the Iraq War, in: The Economist, 03. 04. 2003.

3 *Abbas, Tahir*: Recent Developments to British Multicultural Theory, Policy and Practice. The Case of British Muslims, in: Citizenship Studies, No. 3, Vol. 9, 2005, pp. 153-166.

policy and practice, and not of personal choice, which apparently leads to 'parallel lives' or 'self-styled segregation'. Gatekeepers in the housing market, i. e., estate agents, landlords and 'buy-to-letters', are in the process of selecting in or selecting out certain groups deemed more or less desirable. There is also the role of 'white flight' in relation to majority groups leaving these areas, leading to acceleration in concentration. Clearly there are many more factors to take into account than merely the idea of personal choice – on most occasions, most people simply have no choice.[4] Education and health are two other areas also of particular concern, with certain young Muslim men in the North and in less wealthier areas in the South finding themselves near the bottom of the heap. At the same, Muslim numbers are growing exponentially in schools such as Harrow, Westminster and Eaton.

The wealth of second and third generation Muslims in the South rises rapidly in certain ethnicities, social classes, and, invariably, local areas. We are seeing young Muslim women outperforming young Muslim men at all levels and in all subjects, but these achievements are not always translated into relative representation in higher education. Heath inequalities are also emerging, with perinatal mortality, coronary heart disease, diabetes and angina among the many illnesses affecting Muslims in particular. Call it a function of diet and lifestyle, but it would be wrong to neglect the role of stress on poor and struggling families. And yet, with all the empirical evidence available to us, after the Northern disturbances, not to be called 'riots' as the Home Office wishes to bear no responsibly for what it sees as local uprisings, the notion of 'Community Cohesion' has been bandied about. However, it is a blame-the-victim pathology, with no sense of the deep-seated structural inequalities, racialisms and exclusions facing groups at the heart of problems relating to building stronger forms of social capital.

How can one decrease *unhealthy* bonding, but increase *healthy* bridging and linking social capital without an equal opportunity structure and biting policy to alleviate disadvantage and exclusion? For all of the enthusiasm in relation to 'Community Cohesion', there are few positive outcomes one can get truly excited about. It was a myopic political project at the outset, and remains so in the current period. And, in the process, it has taken race and ethnic relations back to early phase of post-war history and discussions. Instead of focusing on integration, in 2001 'Community Cohesion' attempted to reverse the multiculturalist trend of the time; this reversal emerged in the wake of the Stephen Lawrence murder enquiry and developments to the Race Relations (Amendment) Act 2000. This has been done at major costs.

---

4 *Peach, Ceri*: Muslims in the 2001 Census of England and Wales. Gender and Economic Disadvantage, in: Ethnic and Racial Studies, No. 4, Vol. 29, 2006, pp. 629-655.

Internationally, there are significant concerns that impact the Muslim *Ummah* – to some an amorphous concept, to others a considerable force that generates a global following and transcends nation and ethnicity. Further still, what space of hope is there for Muslims in the aftermath of the terror attacks on the World Trade Centre and the Pentagon in 2001, and the beginning of the 'War on Terror'? This so-called War (there does not seem to be a willing enemy) is, after all, a neo-conservative effort to paint a rickety organisation as a sophisticated, warring machine, operating out of secret underground caves and bunkers in the mountainous regions of Waziristan. This war has no single definable enemy – Bin Laden is one of hundreds of political leaders in the Muslim world who see American and European intervention in Muslims lands as the root of all their problems. And yet it rages on in Afghanistan and Iraq, in the holding cells in Europe ready for an extraordinary rendition, or in the home, with senior politicians fixated on the threat of 'Islamic terrorism' or 'Muslim extremism'. This global war of terror has been led by the USA, but it has Britain in tow.

In the eyes of the 'Arab Street', with Sarkozy joining the gang, the journey from Afghanistan to Iraq to potentially Iran, Syria or even Pakistan is being contemplated. Britain joined the 'War on Terror' at the behest of one man alone, Tony Blair. Having been removed from office in 2007, he lectures the world on faith and globalisation, with his essential question: How can all that is good in the great religions come together to make a stronger world when religion is regarded by some to have been a force for evil, tyranny and despotism, particularly in the twentieth century? It does not take a Yale scholar to answer this question. Illegal wars, control of the flow of the natural resources of the world, and being able to treat disadvantaged, disaffected and disillusioned minorities well at home could lead to many relevant answers.

But it is at home that I want concentrate the remainder of my talk. My home is where we have the strongest anti-discrimination legislation in Western Europe, but we do not have a single high court judge of a non-male, non-white-English background. We do have many peers and MPs, but nowhere near as many as the population profile would suggest. How many Muslim professors are there? How many senior police officers? How many head teachers? Prison governors? Chairs of primary care trusts? I can go on and on... In the post-9/11 and post-7/7 climate, the representation issue could not be more distinctive. Take a random sample of people and ask them to think of a word in their minds after the word Islamic, most would say... TERRORIST! The conflation between Islamic politics, political Islam and the politics of Muslims is found in all sectors of society. All of a sudden, police, social services, local housing, educational authorities, prisons services and security agencies are focused on what it means to be a 'Muslim terrorist', not a Muslim *per se*. As has been the case throughout recent history, the problems are seen as 'Muslim' and *not* societal, which is, effectively, what they are.

The 7/7 bombers, the many foiled attempts, the rising prosecutions of British Muslims involved in terror plots and the current trails in relation to young Muslim men implicated in terror plots all point to one thing. These young men are products of British society. They all have one thing in common: a 'made in Britain' sign stamped across their foreheads. Arguably, many here are faulty products, but their elimination lies in the manufacturing process. Genuine downward social mobility, limitations to aspirations, criminalisation, alienation, exclusion and vilification as well as increased hostility from some sectors of majority society have all led to a generation of young Muslims, particularly in the poorer cut-off areas of the country, North and South, to seek solutions in a violent jihadi intervention. Indeed, Jihad is a concept in Islam – but what does it mean or signify? A struggle, but often the most overlooked and the most significant jihad is against the Ego – *jihad an-nafs* (Sigmund Freud would have a field day if he was still around today). Here, it is important to get the mosques, imams, leadership and women's issues fundamentally right, but we are not going to get there by merely focusing on cultures and values.

It is important that policy and practice concentrate on the fundamental building block of strong and resilient communities: the economic empowerment which leads to social and cultural efficacy. An increase in trust leads to confidence, participation and representation. I have not got enough time to talk about the media, but we do not need to delve to deep to realise the negative impact of a 'Jack Straw what not to wear debate' in October 2006, or that what Dr. Rowan Williams stated in relation to informal Sharia courts in February 2008 has been going on in parts of the country for over fifteen years. The media sensationalises to sell. Good news on Muslims or in relation to Christians, Jews, Hindus and so on simply does not sell. Muslim space in the media is still to find its rightful place. The Orientalism of the old is reinvented in the Islamophobia of the new, and we see it time and time again.

In my final few words I want to stress that there are many challenges facing British Muslims today, but every single one can be turned into an opportunity. For all the failings this society generates, most of its citizens would rather not be anywhere else. Let us try to create a space of hope that does not simply belong to or is merely owned by Muslims alone. Muslims and non-Muslims alike, now is your chance. Thank you for your attention.

References

Abbas, Tahir: Recent Developments to British Multicultural Theory, Policy and Practice. The Case of British Muslims, in: Citizenship Studies, No. 3, Vol. 9, 2005, pp. 153-166

Abbas, Tahir: British Islam. The Road to Radicalism, Cambridge 2009

Peach, Ceri: Muslims in the 2001 Census of England and Wales. Gender and Economic Disadvantage, in: Ethnic and Racial Studies, No. 4, Vol. 29, pp. 629-655

West Europe's Muslims and the Iraq War, in: The Economist, 03. 04. 2003

The Freedom that I Mean ...
or *The Heart – or Wurst – of the Matter*[1]

Necla Kelek

Currently, some 15 million people with non-German cultural backgrounds live in Germany, among them some 3 million Muslims and about 2.4 million people of Turkish origin. Labour immigration was a process that brought advantages to both sides – to the German economy and to the immigrants – even if the circumstances were complicated and the burdens unevenly distributed. Leftist and Green-Party politics saw and still see this immigration as, among other things, a means towards global social redistribution: Immigrants are victims of international exploitation and are therefore to be protected.

The majority of immigrants have, in spite of everything, been integrated or assimilated into German society. On the whole, German society has – barring some minor mistakes and setbacks – achieved a great degree of integration. Just like the Turks, the Greeks, Italians, and Portuguese came as guest workers to Germany, and stayed there. Not all immigrant groups were inclined to withdraw into their own culture and isolate themselves from the rest of society. We must differentiate when speaking of failed integration.

For example, no-one considers the neighbourhood near the jetties at Hamburg's port – most of whose residents are Portuguese – to be a parallel society, even though it is strongly marked by Portuguese culture. With its restaurants, food, music, cultural and sporting organisations, and bilingual schools, it enriches the cultural diversity of the city. It shows that one can maintain one's cultural identity while still being a German citizen. This is completely different from the Muslim enclaves of Hamburg-Wilhelmsburg and Veddel; or certain areas of Berlin into which female police officers are not sent on patrol because they are simply not accepted by the men; or those areas in which Arab clans settle their disputes amongst themselves via self-appointed justices of the peace. The people there see themselves as Muslims, Turks, or Arabs. They identify themselves with their culture and religion in an exclusionary way – the concept of 'cultural enrichment' does not enter the picture here.

There must therefore be something other than immigration status or ethnicity that leads one immigrant to participate in society and another to be excluded from it, something that creates problems primarily with immigrants from the Muslim Turkish and Arab cultural areas. In order to identify this, we must bring certain differences and distinctions to the fore.

1 Translated from the German by Kareem James Abu-Zeid.

This is the difference between cultural diversity and multiculturalism:

> "Multikulturalismus bedeutet ein Leben nebeneinander, also eine Aneinanderreihung von Parallelgesellschaften. Kultureller Pluralismus ein Leben miteinander durch wertebezogene Gemeinsamkeiten."[2]

We can assume that in the coming years – especially in the cities – some 40 % of the population will have a so-called immigrant background. The host society will not be the majority society forever, and if it does not soon agree on the values and forms of coexistence, and convince the immigrants that the values of this society can regulate social life for the good of one and all, then our democracy will be harmed and our social peace endangered. This society will turn into one of groups and parallel societies. I do not believe that anyone wants this.

The moment of truth has come. *Es geht um die Wurst*, as the German saying goes: We have come to the heart – literally, the sausage or wurst – of the matter. I mean this in more than one sense here. For one thing, I mean it in the sense that the cultural question will determine our future.

I also mean 'the heart', or rather wurst, of the matter as food, as a sign of cultural difference and different culinary practices, especially as they are expressed via other worldviews and views on the human, through other traditions and religious representations, and especially other value systems. But before I talk about sausages and explain what they have to do with Islam, let me speak about something simple and seemingly self-evident: freedom.

Freedom Is Not for Us Women

I have now been living in Germany for forty years. I spent the first ten years of my life in Istanbul and in a village in Anatolia. I left my parents' home when I was 19, and have been a German citizen since 1994. I am at home in two cultures: I was socialised in a Turkish-Muslim family; yet I was educated in German society, where I learned critical thinking and interdisciplinary discourse. As a young girl, I used to sit at the window and watch others ride bicycles, without being allowed to ride one myself. It was a long way from that young girl to the lecturer who, in 1990 and as a *Wessi*, a West German, went to Greifswald in former East Germany to enthusiastically teach civil servants of the Ministry of State Security the meaning of Western values and freedoms.

2 "Multiculturalism means living in juxtaposition to one another, and thus a stringing-together of parallel societies. Cultural pluralism means coexistence by drawing on common values." *Tibi, Bassam*: Islamische Zuwanderung. Die gescheiterte Integration, 2nd edition, Stuttgart/München 2002, p. 184.

For me, 'freedom' meant something very special. And also something new, for the meaning of the German word (*Freiheit*), namely 'being independent', is not a value in Muslim Turkish upbringing. As a child, I learned of freedom only as something foreign, something reserved for the men. In Muslim Turkish society, the child is not raised as an individual, as an autonomous person, but rather as a social entity that must first obey and serve the family and community – especially if that child is a girl. It is not the individual, but rather the community that is the defining factor in Turkish culture, and especially Muslim culture in general. The collective is placed above the individual. The individual is considered part of the family, the clan, the country. Group objectives therefore have greater significance in the Turkish Constitution than protection of the individual. Similarly, Turkish and Muslim associations attempt to assert their interests as groups – I will say more about this later.

'*Hürriyet*' means 'freedom' in Turkish. The word is derived from the Arabic concept *hurriya,*[3] which originally meant the opposite of slavery, and not that which in the Western tradition is associated with 'libertas', namely the emancipation of the individual from the yoke of tutelage and subservience, including religious subservience. *Hurriya* means that a slave becomes 'free' to serve God. For devout Muslims, freedom in this sense consists of the conscious decision 'to obey the prescriptions of Islam'. The Islamic associations also understand the basic right of 'freedom of religion' in this way, namely as the right to obey Islam in this country. The fact that this view is so radically different from what is understood by the European concept of freedom is a sign of cultural difference.

When I, as a young girl, asked my mother when I would be free, meaning when I could decide for myself what I want to do, she replied: "Freedom was not made for us." She did not even understand my question. For her, 'being free' was the same as being an outlaw, i. e. being without protection. 'Being free' means being unprotected, abandoned. In case of doubt, the woman is surrendered to male violence. Men protect the women from the violence of strange men. If one's husband is violent, that is one's kismet, one's fate. In the lives of Muslim women, men are protectors and guardians. Men are the public sphere, and women their private sphere.

For Muslim women, there is only freedom 'from something': freedom from the hostility of strangers, but also freedom from taking responsibility for themselves, freedom from their own will. You may object that this is the exception, and you certainly know women who are Muslim yet independent. Yes, I say, that too is true.

I am not, however, talking about individual cases, but rather about the values of a religion and a culture. Even in the Koran, Islamic culture does not guarantee women equal rights, but rather only equal dignity. And even in the published draft of the as yet incomplete Turkish Constitution commissioned by the AKP Govern-

3 *Diner, Dan*: Versiegelte Zeit. Über den Stillstand in der islamischen Welt, Berlin 2005, p. 52.

ment, women are not to have equal rights but rather, like children and the disabled, are to be placed 'under special protection'. This 'protection' is ultimately nothing other than paternalism, tutelage, and the paraphrasing of a property claim. It is thus the opposite of civil liberty.

Of course, there are women who have succeeded in escaping this cultural system, a system that is at odds with the needs of modern society and that thwarts the hopes of women in the present day. And luckily, our society offers this opportunity. However, those who have managed to win their freedom forget the others all too quickly and speak of their freedom as if it were a matter of course for everyone. I myself have escaped from these constraints, and many other women have perhaps also done so – yet this cultural character remains and is being reproduced. The figures are clear. Muslim women in general are married young and have no money at their disposal; they work less, are subject to more domestic violence, and are less independent than comparable groups.

We are dealing with a dominant culture that follows Muslim concepts, and whose supreme principle is obedience to God, yet also obedience to God's representatives: the state, the elders, the husband, or even the brother. As a religion of revelation and of law, Islam claims to regulate all aspects of life. It does not recognise, as the historian Dan Diner writes, the "Prozeß ständiger Interpretation, Verhandlung und Verwandlung dessen, was entweder ins Innere der Person verlegt oder nach außen hin entlassen und durch etablierte Institutionen reguliert wird".[4]

We have to bear this in mind when comparing cultural values. We are speaking of different things while using the same terms and concepts. Freedom, decency, dignity, honour, shame, respect, dialogue: Certain definitions are bound up with all of these terms in Western-European society, yet they have very different definitions in the Islamic-Turkish-Arabic culture. We need something like an Islam-German, German-Islam dictionary to name all these differences.

Haram Means Sin

I had to win my freedom; otherwise I never would have gotten it. And now I am finally bringing the wurst, the sausage, into the picture. I was 18 years old – and thus an adult – and in the last year of my training as an engineering draughtswoman, when I gathered up all my courage on the way home from work to do something that I had decided on a long time ago: to eat a sausage. A bratwurst. Only the *gavur*, the unbelievers, ate bratwurst, for bratwurst consists mainly of pork – and pork is *haram*, forbidden. I thus ordered the wurst, hesitated, and expected that either the earth would open up and swallow me or that I would be struck by lightning with

4 "The process of constant interpretation, negotiation, and transformation of that which is either transferred to the inner psyche of a person or outwardly discharged and regulated through established institutions"; ibid.

the first bite. The bratwurst was not particularly tasty, but the important thing was that *nothing happened.* No earthquake, no inner hellfire, nothing. None of the stuff that I had been taught to fear as a child happened. Something must have been wrong with the system of fear. From that point on, I had a secret that I shared with no-one. I had sinned, and I felt good doing it, and suspected that it would perhaps be the same with other forbidden things. I felt, perhaps, like a modern-day girl who had lost her innocence.

As harmless as this anecdote sounds, it is exemplary for the socialisation of many Muslim children. They are raised by means of 'poisonous pedagogy' – i. e. by means of fear and often violence – to become social beings who are obedient to the community, i. e. to the elders, the husbands, the uncles, the brothers, the mothers-in-law. The permissible and the forbidden, the pure and the unclean are defined very precisely. Raising children to be independent and responsible for themselves is not the goal.

Yes, I had won the freedom to commit a sin, a sin I had been too scared to commit for quite a long time. I needed another thirty years to be able to speak about it in public. Freedom, a concept we take to be self-evident, is frightening to many women. They fear freedom because they do not know it. They do not know what it means to be free and independent, what it means to bear responsibility for oneself. Whoever has it beaten into them from childhood that they are supposed to be obedient, whoever sees nothing except their own four walls – those people will at some point be afraid of making their own decisions, even if it is something as simple as taking a walk in the woods or going to the doctor alone. To say nothing of how these people, who have never learned to bear responsibility for themselves, are to become conscious, responsible citizens who are supposed to have a say in the decisions of the state.

I thus vehemently encourage children, regardless of where they come from, to do as much as possible on their own. I encourage them to try out for themselves swimming, climbing, going to museums and theatres. And I believe that they should be prevented from 'freely' putting on a headscarf – they must first learn to be autonomous and think independently. Intellectual and corporal autonomy are, together with a good education, the prerequisites for freedom.

Freedom must be learned. And our schools are there to teach it to them, in addition to everything else. I am thus also against childcare benefits, because I would like for all children to come into contact not only with the German language but also with the German culture of self-awareness and independence as early as possible, i. e. in kindergarten. And they cannot do this with a mother from Anatolia who speaks no German and knows nothing about this society.

The German language is a very important means of integration; without the language, there can be no education and no participation. Yet if it is limited to linguistic education, integration will not succeed at giving people an identity, a self-consciousness as democratic citizens.

What Is Respect

But allow me to provide another example of that cultural difference that I view as a decisive obstacle to integration, another example of the necessity of a consensus regarding social norms. In the Muslim Turkish canon of values, 'respect' plays a large role. Respect of one's elders, of those stronger than oneself, of religion, of Turkey, of the father, the uncle, the brother. When an *abi* – an older brother – demands 'respect' from a younger brother or a stranger, he is demanding a gesture of humility. Even grown-up sons, for example, only speak or smoke in the presence of their fathers and uncles when invited to do so; they subordinate themselves, and thus show their elders 'respect'. This is an absolute orientation towards those higher up in the hierarchy, towards a patriarchal system. Thus, 'respect' means nothing other than submission and is quite equal to the meaning of the term 'Islam'. Islam literally means submission and devotion. Showing respect means recognising the existing power relations, which implies accepting the principles of this religion. The members of the group, the family, the clan, etc, are not equal, but are rather to be respected according to their sex, age, and rank. Rebelling against an elder is, in this religious cultural system, akin to rebelling against the divine order.

It is unthinkable for a girl to express her opinion to her elders or even to her husband. I have seen sons who are about twelve years old go shopping with their mothers and hold the wallet in their hands to pay, because the boy, as the eldest man in the house in the absence of the father, is the authority. The hierarchy is not the result of any natural authority, but rather is defined in terms of age and sex, and these are God-given.

Something similar happens socially, and also with regards to faith. It is necessary to show 'respect' for the prophets and the religion, and criticism or drawing cartoons about them is not allowed, because neither Muslims nor unbelievers have the right to call the divine order into question. It is not only that one is not allowed to call this order into question, one also does not have the right to pose any questions other than simple ones asking for explanations. Asking critical questions means doubting. And doubt is seen as sacrilege and has been banished from Islamic doctrine since the 12th century. The Turkish Prime Minister Tayyip Erdogan reduced this to the following conclusive statement: "Our religion is free of errors." With this remark, the Turkish Prime Minister finds himself, from a theological standpoint, back in the 7th century.

In Verse 110 of Sura 3, Allah has Mohammed say: "You are the greatest community that was ever made for men; you command what is right and forbid what is wrong, and you believe in God." Worldly events are therefore not to be determined by man, but rather should follow Allah's authority. In a society marked by Islam, one must 'show respect' for the God-given order. The older brother appeals to God when he gives his sister orders. And the mother appeals to this order when she marries off her daughter. You have certainly noticed that I am attempting to speak about Western values by presenting you with Islamic cultural norms that are either irreconcilable with them or that would – if one were to accept them unquestioned – deeply alter our coexistence.

When we speak of 'respect' according to Western value measurements, we mean mutual consideration, and also 'acceptance'. One must 'earn respect'. The American sociologist Richard Sennett describes 'respect' as a social instrument of mutual consideration that is manifested in behaviour, rituals, and not least in both laws and the consideration of those needs of other people that are not the same as one's own.[5] And Jürgen Habermas describes the consideration of dissenting opinions that arise from other interests.

Sennett formulates three main ideas on which society can mould people's characters in order to foster mutual respect:

1. The development of one's own abilities and skills.

2. Caring for oneself.

3. Striving to give others something back.

Or, to express it more concisely:

Make something of yourself! Take care of yourself! Help others!

This principle of self-responsibility is extremely suspicious to Muslims. They consider individualism to be egotism. What we have to be clear about when reflecting on our identity as Europeans is that the achievements of our culture – and also our social life itself – are being called into question *not* via other sets of beliefs or certain forms of spirituality, but rather via a different political and social ideal, a different worldview and a different concept of man. This other culture is simply not tolerant. Rather, it claims to be tolerant in order to promote itself. Wherever it holds the majority, or where Muslims are able to act assertively, these freedoms gradually disappear. I could now demonstrate this with a host of examples, but I would like to limit myself to one, because it elucidates the relation between history, faith, politics, and everyday life via a single thing.

5 *Sennett, Richard*: Respekt im Zeitalter der Ungleichheit, Berlin 2002.

The Heart – or *Wurst* – of the Matter

For Muslims, pigs are monsters, and everything to do with pigs is unclean. This reasoning goes so far that gummi bears were declared 'unclean' because parts of pigs are allegedly used in their preparation. I was invited, together with a group of Muslim women, to attend a Christmas event hosted by the Evangelical Church; yet the women stayed away from the gathering because pork might have been prepared in the church kitchen. On Turkish state television, the series 'Winnie the Pooh' is not allowed to be broadcast because 'Piglet' is in it, and this might confuse the children and insult Muslim sensibilities. 'The Three Little Pigs' as well as 'Miss Piggy' from the 'Muppet Show' are kept away from Muslim children – in Pakistan, Miss Piggy is even on the wanted-persons list of the guardian of public morals. And banks frequented by Muslim customers do not distribute piggy banks on World Savings Day, but rather penny banks in the form of elephants.

This aversion is justified by using the Koran. In it, we can read several almost identical verses: "Forbidden to you are dead meat, blood, pork, and that which was slaughtered with an invocation to any other than God" (The Koran, Sura 5, 'The Table', Verse 3).

It is commonly argued that the origin of this prescription is justified by the fact that the pig is a dirty animal and can transmit, among other things, trichinosis. This is a myth. This parasite was first discovered in 1835 and its pathogens only pass from the animal to humans when meat is undercooked. Cows, sheep, and goats can transmit it just as well as pigs. If we were dealing with a hygienic prescription, then hyenas should also have been banned from the historical menus of the first Muslims, for they nourish themselves exclusively with dead meat. Yet the Islamic legal schools consider them to be, along with lizards, edible. Moreover – and this should make one suspicious – pigs are not native to the Arabian desert. Pigs were largely unknown to the Arabs because they provided no milk, fur, or wool, but rather only meat, and in addition to this could be used neither as draught animals nor as mounts. Nor were the nomads interested in them from an economic point of view. Mohammed could therefore label pigs 'abominations' without any consequences, because they were only important to the unbelievers in the north and thus represented – and still represent – an easy means of differentiation.

Yet no-one is demanding that Muslims eat sausages or knuckles of pork. Everyone is allowed to abstain from the consumption of certain things on religious grounds or on grounds of taste. But – and now we are getting at the crux of the problem, and that which most directly concerns us – no-one should be considered a worse person because of their culinary preferences. When Muslims use 'pigs' to define themselves as 'clean' and define pork-eaters as 'unclean' and then refuse contact with their German neighbours because of this, we are not dealing with religion or religious sentiments, but rather with the discrimination of people of different faiths –

we are dealing with religious apartheid. This is the attempt, in many fields, to establish the 'religious life' of Muslims as a norm that is to be accepted, and thus an attempt at desecularising life in our country. The debates about headscarves and the construction of mosques are only a part of this religious-political struggle, one that is being led by Muslims behind the veil of religious freedom.

Within the scope of this presentation, I can only suggest that with regards to the debate over the Islamic consensus of values, we are not dealing with problems that one 'need only clarify in order to understand'. The representatives of integration and the patrons of Islam have long worked as if this were the case, have asked Muslims about Islamic values in order to facilitate an 'arrival' for Muslims in this society. Yet when we look closely, and my examples are only a small part of a giant veil that lies over this culture, we will understand that we are dealing with a conflict of values that reaches to the very foundations of our social life and that will change Europe if we do not commit to a distinctly European identity.

For some time now, this conflict has been the topic of the 'German Islam Conference' in which I have been participating on the invitation of the Ministry of the Interior. For almost a year, we have been discussing a joint statement on the consensus of values with Islamic associations.

The contentious text reads as follows:

> "Grundlage ist neben unseren Wertvorstellungen und unserem kulturellen Selbstverständnis unsere freiheitliche und demokratische Ordnung, wie sie sich aus der deutschen und europäischen Geschichte entwickelt hat und im Grundgesetz ihre verfassungsrechtliche Ausprägung findet."[6]

The Islamic associations of the Coordinating Council of Muslims refuse to agree to this formulation.

It seems incomprehensible that the functionaries of Islam do not want to agree to this self-evident formulation, yet there is a simple reason for this: They mistrust the values of freedom and self-responsibility. They say that they stand by the Constitution, yet by this they mean only the right to religious freedom. They are referring to their right to live their faith as a group, and not the right to freedom of religion per se or to the freedom of the individual. In the statutes of the Muslim Coordinating Council, they have committed themselves to the dominant culture of 'Koran and Sunna'. They accept the Constitution, but do not want to animate it. They have problems with this because the religion of Islam has never been secularised – politics and religion are all the same to them.

6 "In addition to our moral concepts and our cultural self-understanding, our free and democratic structures form our foundation, because they have developed out of German and European history and found their juridical expression in the Constitution."

Islam acknowledges no hierarchy, no clergy, no binding doctrines, but rather only tradition. Yet even the Koran contradicts itself, and Muslims often disagree about how to approach it. The Sunna, i. e. the example of Mohammed, is nothing other than traditions and customs that have become ideology. Nevertheless, the representatives of each organisation speak for 'Islam', and maintain that no problem – from terrorism to coercion to failed integration, depending on the situation at hand – has 'anything to do with Islam'. There are no obligations in this worldview, and therefore there is also no sense of responsibility. "Der Islam ist das, was man daraus macht",[7] Bassam Tibi says. Or as I would express it: Islam is what the functionaries of Islam pass it off as at any given time. For me, Islam, as a worldview and a system of values, cannot be integrated into European society and therefore should not be recognised as a public body. It is not a question of good will. Islam cannot be integrated. The institutional, structural, and theological prerequisites for it are missing, and its representatives lack, as Habermas says, "eine in Überzeugung verwurzelte Legitimation"[8].

Islam cannot be integrated, but the individual Muslim *can* be integrated as a citizen. He can preserve both his faith and his identity in our society, for the tolerance of the European Enlightenment considers members of all religions, as well as dissenters, to have equal rights; it exiles faith to the private sphere, because the public sphere is secular.

One of Islam's fundamental problems is the lack of separation between the state and religion. This lack of separation became Muslim state tradition with the introduction of orthodoxy in the year 847, at the latest. In Christian societies, the separation of religion and the state took place in the course of the Enlightenment. The 'making worldly' of a society is understood under the term 'secularisation'. The Latin *saeculum* means century, a limited period of time, one with a beginning and an end. Secularism historically indicates the transition from 'eternal' to 'temporal' values. Values – and also articles of faith – were thus seen in their historical context for the first time, were opened up to the historicising gaze. They could be discarded or re-established, could rise and fall. This development was labelled 'the Enlightenment'. It brought the concept of freedom into the world. Man-made law took the place of God's law. In place of a fate determined by God, man was now endowed with reason, and could take his fate into his own hands. 'Enlightenment', the "light of reason", as the English philosopher John Locke named it, enabled man to cognitively penetrate those fateful environments that were hitherto incomprehensible, and to orient himself intellectually. True Enlightenment is thus also the Enlightenment of man with regards to his boundaries and the recognition that man is an autonomous creator of this world and does not serve merely as the executor of otherworldly prescriptions.

7 "Islam is what one makes of it."

8 "A legitimation rooted in conviction."

Faith was not done away with, not even among the Christians. But from now on, God was no longer 'the Law', but rather the creator and preserver of the world, one who had – and I'm citing the Bible, not the Koran here – "crowned men with mercy and compassion." According to Christian understanding, every man is an image of God:

> "Niemals darf dieser Mensch zum bloßen Objekt für fremde Zwecke, zum bloßen Gegenstand der Verfügungsansprüche Anderer werden. Der von Kant unter dem Titel der menschlichen Würde formulierte Gedanke, dass der Mensch niemals bloß als Mittel, sondern stets zugleich als Zweck in sich selbst zu betrachten ist, hat hier seine Wurzel."[9]

These thoughts have not reached Islam, and since there is no theology, no historical-critical science in Islam, enlightened minds will always remain dissidents in this religion. It thus seems all the more necessary to me that European society makes sure of its values, that it always questions them, confirms or changes them. The encounter with Islam may make finding this identity easier, since we can work off of a counter-model. My dominant culture has developed itself as a counter-model to the patriarchal-hierarchical religious group identity of Islamic culture. We cannot wait until they reconcile themselves with reason. We cannot wait until Islam is strong enough to doubt itself.

I am proud to live in this country. I am proud of my freedom as a European. As much as (to quote Alfred Grosser) the "German vice of self-pity" annoys me, I am still extremely proud to take part in the debates about German history and the problem of coexistence. This is true freedom, and it seems to me that it represents a part of the true wealth of this society. The fact that we are here today, that we are arguing, that we are grappling with the future of our society, that this is even possible – all of this is a part of 'my' dominant culture... and perhaps also a part of yours. It is a reason to be proud.

9 "This man should never become a mere object for foreign ends, a mere object at the disposal of others. The thought formulated by Kant under the title of human dignity – i. e. that man is never to be viewed merely as a means, but rather always also as an end in himself – has its roots here." *Huber, Wolfgang*: Flugblätter der Freiheit. Verantwortliches Handeln aus christlichen Wurzeln. Weiße Rose – Gedächtnisvorlesung in der Ludwig-Maximilians-Universität München; http://staatskirchenrecht.de/vortraege/huber/060123_huber_weisse_rose.html [15. 10. 2010].

References

Diner, Dan: Versiegelte Zeit. Über den Stillstand in der islamischen Welt, Berlin 2005

Huber, Wolfgang: Flugblätter der Freiheit. Verantwortliches Handeln aus christlichen Wurzeln. Weiße Rose – Gedächtnisvorlesung in der Ludwig-Maximilians-Universität München; http://staatskirchenrecht.de/vortraege/huber/060123_huber_weisse_rose.html [15. 10. 2010]

Sennett, Richard: Respekt im Zeitalter der Ungleichheit, Berlin 2002

Tibi, Bassam: Islamische Zuwanderung. Die gescheiterte Integration, 2nd edition, Stuttgart/ München 2002

Muslim Women Between Emancipation and Self-Denial[1]

Serap Çileli

The deeper cause of today's integration deficit is, among other things, the religious and traditional – i. e. patriarchal-authoritarian – upbringing of Muslim children. It is girls from the Muslim culture group who suffer under this rigid and outdated familial structure, and the problematic that results from it often remains invisible and unheard. The fear of estrangement from Islam and from the traditional culture of origin is still deeply anchored in the Muslim consciousness. The fathers and sons of these families see to it that their daughters and sisters fit into traditional female roles. This obligation to obedience to one's parents and elders, together with a stubborn virginity myth, force Muslim girls and women into an overly rigid and formal straitjacket of dictated femininity. Contact with Germans is limited to a minimum and having a boyfriend or sex before marriage is out of the question. It is also taboo to spend their very restricted leisure time outside of the home. They are reduced to the role of the mother and the 'true housewife'; this, along with religious devotion and reverence to Allah, is all they have left. The parents send their children to a nearby mosque to solidify Islamic values in Koran courses, and the girls must submit to wearing the headscarf during their visits to the mosque. The headscarf, which has repeatedly been declared an obligation by imams of Islamic associations, symbolises female submission to male dominance. Many Islamic organisations call on parents to send their daughters to the mosques and Koran courses with the headscarf on – even during the summer holidays, and sometimes as early as primary school. If the Muslim daughters do not comply, they are considered whores and 'fair game'. Girls who do not submit are punished, sometimes to the point of murder in the name of honour.

The Islamic educational methods of Muslim parents – and also those of the Koran classes of the various Islamic associations – are often accompanied by corporal punishment, and promote the isolation of Muslim children and youth. A study by the Turkish sociologist Uslucan on Educational Methods of Turkish Families in Germany showed that violence in the upbringing of children is more common among families of Turkish origin than among German families. In Germany, 20 % of all Turkish families are brought up with violence. This means that every fifth kid of Turkish origin is beaten![2]

---

1 Translated from the German by Kareem James Abu-Zeid.

2 *Kresta, Edith/Wierth, Alke*: "Das Fleisch ist deins". Interview mit Haci Halil Uslucan, in: taz Online, 13. 01. 2003; http://www.taz.de/index.php?id=archivseite&dig=2003/01/13/a0165 [15. 10. 2010].

A widespread phobia among Muslim parents is that their children will become 'Germanised' if they stay or move around in a German milieu. Many parents are even of the opinion that the schools and day-care centres want to assimilate the children into German culture and alienate them from their own culture – and especially from their religion. At home, Muslim culture is imparted to them. Outside, in the kindergartens or at school, they are given German values and norms. Culturally and socially, they swing to and fro, without a goal.

These demands on the youth make integration more difficult – not easier – since the cultural distance between the country of origin and the host society is quite large, and since the two worlds stand in opposition to each other. As a result, the children and grandchildren of the first generation are, as a rule, always seeking recognition in their balancing act between two cultures. Linguistically and culturally, they are caught between two stools.

The problems that result from this are at the centre of the integration problem, and can neither be hushed up nor overlooked. A tension arises here, a burden that falls most severely on children and younger people. For many Muslim youths, this means suspicions, fears, conflicts of conscience, identity problems, and impediments to self-discovery. The potential for conflict that becomes evident here can lead to, among other things, failing school, social isolation, suicide, and behavioural disorders; it can lead to a fall into criminality, to violence, aggressive behaviour, addiction problems, or breakdowns. In this regard, Islamic education, or rather Islamic customs – which demand that the youth blindly obey and subordinate themselves to the powerful head of the family and to one's elders – abandon modern education. The fathers of families adhere to traditional Islamic prescriptions, ideas, and norms; they still possess the consciousness of primitive tribes, deliberately isolating themselves and finding fault with our Western values, which they condemn and hold in contempt.

Against this backdrop, the idea to have Muslim imams go on patrol in the future, to have them act as referees between police officers and criminal Muslim youth, is nothing other than a symbol of the willingness to tolerate a parallel society. Yet with a parallel legal system such as sharia, would a parallel society allow for integration? It may be in the interests of the political and religious groups of the Muslim minority population – or those of Muslim parents – to cut their children off from the society that surrounds them and raise them in opposition to Western values. But the question is: Is it in the interest of the German state to support such intentions?

Living in a Parallel World – Without a Chance for Integration?

The educational problem is without a doubt one of the most important matters that confronts Turkish citizens living in Germany. Statistics show that even third-generation Turkish schoolchildren who have a German passport do not, nationally, have the success that one would hope for. They are clearly overrepresented in special schools. 20 % quit school without a degree. Some 40 % receive a degree from a *Hauptschule*, which is the most common degree among this group. Over half have no intermediate or secondary degree. The number of Turkish university alumni and the number of Turkish students who attend university is proportionately low in comparison to both German students and other foreign students. Language, the basic prerequisite of successful integration, is the fundamental problem of Turkish children. This is especially true among women, whose lives are mainly played out in the familial clan's field of vision. Turks in Germany, for example in large cities, mostly only speak Turkish at home; and many children do not attend kindergarten at all, and thus only begin to learn German in the first grade. It is extremely difficult to make up for the resulting semilingualism, for these children's German-language deficits. Young people with immigrant backgrounds who do not have a school degree and/or who have not completed any vocational training are hard to integrate into both the labour market and society. Disadvantaged youths who lack parental support and do not receive professional orientation or vocational preparation through their parents and schools have no prospects for the future. They develop incredible frustration and envy, a hatred for their environment that cultivates a propensity to violence. The possibility of a criminal career thus emerges.

A typical example is the Turkish youth who beat up an old man in the Munich underground. He had committed a long list of crimes, yet until that moment – December 20, 2007 – his criminal acts had not led to any consequences. It is known that frustration and hatred lead, sooner or later, to rebellion. These feelings of revolt are an ideal breeding ground for Islamic ideologies, as well as for nationalistic ones.

Numerous Islamic institutions compete to give Muslim children an Islamic identity in Germany, for example Islamic schools (e. g. in Berlin, Bonn, Hamburg, Cologne, Mainz, Munich, Nuremberg, and Stuttgart), Islamic weekend schools, Islamic kindergartens, mosques, or private Koran courses.

One thing is certain: Politically motivated Islam has long been making an empire for itself. Muslim claims for the education sector and Muslim tendencies within it are now supported by all democratic political parties, and by the churches. There are also, however, a number of other Islamic and nationalist groups in the German Federal Republic that hold sway over Islamic educational institutions and Koran courses:

The right-wing extremist 'Grey Wolves' – or the 'Nurculuk Movement' – are one prominent example, yet there are still no noteworthy studies on them. The members of the MHP 'Nationalist Movement Party', better known as 'Grey Wolves', idolise the founder of the Nationalist Movement Party as a *Führer*. The first Führer, namely the 'Head Wolf' or 'Lead Wolf', was Alparslan Türkes. The current Führer of the Nurcu-Brotherhood is Fethullah Gülen. The followers of this Turkish preacher are conservative, nationalistic, and puritanical intellectuals and businessmen. In the last 20 to 30 years, Gülen has built up foundations and charitable institutions across the world (including Germany), as well as Islamic media and education networks. We urgently need to ask ourselves: What are these institutions' intentions and how do they go about their work?

Apparently, these institutions are justifying and thus legalising the Islamisation of Germany (and of Europe) via the notion of religious freedom, with the tacit toleration of the German state.

Many cities in Germany (and Europe) are firmly under the sway of Islamic brotherhoods that mould their social environment both culturally and religiously. Men clothed in the manner of Muslim orthodoxy, veiled girls and women, full-bearded *hocas*, Islamic banners and posters – today, all of these leave their mark on the streets of Germany (and Europe).

To all appearances, politically-religiously motivated Muslims are not concerned with the integration of Muslims into the majority society, but rather with non-Muslims adapting themselves to a parallel society. Despite this harsh reality, for years people in Germany were persuaded into believing that a large majority of Muslims were peaceable, and the number of violent Islamists was estimated at ca. 30,000 people. A current study on Muslims in Germany sheds light on the basic truth about conservative Muslims who are ready to use violence. Focus Online notes that 40 % have a fundamentalist orientation, 6 % are ready to use violence. 14 % of those surveyed, of whom almost 40 % have a German passport, are against democracy and accept violence for religious reasons. 12 % identify themselves with a strong religious-moral critique of Western societies, and support corporal punishment and even capital punishment.[3]

3 Viele junge Muslime neigen zur Gewalt, in: Focus Online, 20. 12. 2007; http://www.focus.de/politik/deutschland/studie_aid_230297.html [15. 10. 2010].

Schäuble's study on Muslims brings another truth to light, one that has been stubbornly denied to this very day, namely: that education, German citizenship, or perfect knowledge of the language does *not* protect one from a propensity to violence. According to the study, more than 8 % of Muslim university students thus distance themselves from democracy, and some 6 % of them are both sceptical of democracy *and* supporters of sharia.[4] These facts alone prove that considering linguistic deficits, poor education levels among Muslims, low social status, or unemployment as the sole causes of the Muslim population's lack of integration into the Federal Republic would be too one-sided and superficial. These are only influencing factors, for they are coupled with religious values and cultural norms – as well as with a certain mentality – that contribute to the lack of integration.

The process of the social disintegration of the Turkish-Muslim minority is determined by the dominance of nationalistic Islamist organisations and communities. One must not forget the influence of Turkish spokespersons, academics, members of parliament, businessmen, and media representatives. They all preach the superiority of their own people, their own culture and religion – in this case, Islam. This disintegration, which is desired by the majority of Muslims and controlled by their self-appointed lawyers or spokespersons, together with the spread of chauvinistic and religious extremism, offers us a threatening perspective for the future of the enlightened West. Islamic criminal law is what separates us. That is to say: the strict rules of sharia that regulate the entire political, social, cultural, and personal life of the Muslim *ummah*. Here, the rules from the seventh century are still in force. Since Islam is so tightly bound up with the laws of sharia, it is incompatible with our democratic system of laws. It is respect for human rights and basic freedoms, as well as cultural adaptation to the local majority society, that binds us together, and that constitutes one of the prerequisites of successful integration.

In Conclusion, an Appeal to All Democrats

We must emphatically support humanist and Enlightenment values, which are the basis of Western civilisation. To avoid a fall back into barbarism, we must adhere to the principles of equality and justice, humanity and tolerance. Whoever calls for a 'reversal of values' is falling right into the trap that the Islamic fundamentalists have set for us. This state, which is governed by the rule of law, cannot tolerate two different laws and partially accept sharia, for this would ultimately lead to a 'state within a state'.

4 *Reimann, Anna*: Schäubles Muslim-Studie. 500 Seiten politischer Sprengstoff, in: Spiegel Online, 20. 12. 2007; http://www.spiegel.de/politik/deutschland/0,1518,524535,00.html [15. 10. 2010].

References

Kresta, Edith/Wierth, Alke: "Das Fleisch ist deins". Interview mit Haci Halil Uslucan, in: taz Online, 13. 01. 2003; http://www.taz.de/index.php?id=archivseite&dig=2003/01/13/a0165 [15. 10. 2010]

Reimann, Anna: Schäubles Muslim-Studie. 500 Seiten politischer Sprengstoff, in: Spiegel Online, 20. 12. 2007; http://www.spiegel.de/politik/deutschland/0,1518,524535,00.html [15. 10. 2010]

Viele junge Muslime neigen zur Gewalt, in: Focus Online, 20. 12. 2007; http://www.focus.de/politik/deutschland/studie_aid_230297.html [15. 10. 2010]

A Minority Perspective on the EU's Commitment to Promoting Anti-Discrimination Policies

Bashy Quraishy

At this very particular moment in the history of the European continent, the anti-racist movement badly needs researchers, academics, intellectuals and decision makers who could and should help combine activism with proper guidance, sound analysis and solid documentation, which can be useful in public debates.

Talking about anti-racism in Europe from an NGO's perspective on this issue is subjective but hopefully informative. In this attempt, I can make use of my long association with the European Network Against Racism – ENAR – in order to elaborate on how it is helping protect minorities in the European Union. No description of anti-discrimination in the EU would be complete without looking at the efforts of the EU Commission and what the EU's own anti-discrimination policy has achieved to this point and in which direction we are all heading. To do so, it is imperative that we look at the situation of racism and discrimination across this humanist, tolerant and democratic continent. An overview of the situation would help put things in the right perspective. This will require that I be honest and straightforward, and that I bring out into the open the worries and difficulties that diverse ethnic and religious groups are experiencing nowadays. One may not agree with my assessments, but they can be the basis of a dialogue.

As far as racism in Europe is concerned, we are definitely heading in the wrong direction. This is even more alarming when it comes to the treatment of non-European minorities, especially those of Islamic backgrounds. On top of this, we are facing a revival of anti-Semitism, and more information is also surfacing regarding an age-old phenomenon, namely the exclusion of the Roma people.

Whichever way one looks at the present European continent, one can hear, see and read a very frightening trend emerging in political, social, legal and public fields. To top it all, the media is playing a special role, not only in spreading prejudices but also in fanning the flames of racism through its irresponsible coverage and its focus on the ethnicity, cultures, religions and traditions of minority groups. Every individual of non-European background is considered a representative of his or her group. An example is the use of the word 'Muslim' in front of or after an individual or a negative action. For example: Islamic terrorism, Islamic militants, Muslim Turks, Moroccan Muslim dress, etc. The list is long. And this rhetoric is constantly escalating. Public opinion polls confirm the dire consequences of such mass hysteria and a significant shift in political trends. There are very few voices of reason being raised to counter this development.

The EU and Racism

Looking at racism in a wider historical context, we can see that, from the 1957 Rome Treaty until the signing of the Amsterdam Treaty of 1997, there was not a single word in any agreement, treaty or directive concerning racial discrimination in the labour market, in social and health services, in housing or in education, nor was there any mention of violence against immigrants and refugees. It was not until June 1997 that the heads of state in the EU gave in to the demands of NGOs and inserted into the Amsterdam Treaty an anti-discrimination clause commonly known as Article 13, thus paving the way for anti-discrimination directives. That happened largely due to the efforts of some very committed Irish NGOs who in 1996 convinced their politicians that an anti-discrimination clause was a must in the treaty that was being drafted and that later came to be known as the Amsterdam Treaty.

The result of this dramatic development was that, for the first time, non-European persons were to receive some legal protection – some justice for all the taxes they had paid, all the labour they had offered and all the injustices they had experienced over the past decades. But what European systems gave with one hand, they are taking away with the other. What do I mean by that? I simply mean that while the EU is making efforts to curb racial discrimination, most countries in Europe are becoming safe havens for cultural and religious racism.

Once again, we see all over Europe a process of demonisation taking hold that is not just about Black and White. Today it is not skin colour that is the main reference point for discrimination. Even Swedish Skinheads, Danish Nazis, Italian Fascists and French Nationalists have toned down their insistence about a hierarchy of races and scientific racism. Now, race and ethnicity arguments have been replaced by the presence of cultures, civilisations and religions from outside Europe.

Having said that, it is also worth remembering that those forces that have set this agenda in motion are not ignorant, stupid or even evil. They know that to uphold a 'Fortress Europe', they cannot play the race card as they once did. That is why the threat from a coloured immigrant has been redefined as the threat of the bogus asylum seeker, an economic refugee, a culturally backward immigrant and of course, the Islamic terrorist who hates the Western way of life and wants to destroy it. This rising tide of Islamophobia and anti-Semitism in Europe are clear signs that racism is taking a different course. In many countries, it is now an officially sanctioned and publicly accepted reality, and one that is being advanced by the media.

Unfortunately, anti-racist movements in Europe are not taking this shift in attitudes and practices seriously because they are thinking about or looking at the bigger picture. They, or at least most of them, still hold firmly to the notion of arranging demonstrations, printing posters and shouting slogans. Not that there is anything wrong with this old-fashioned anti-racist work. But it is high time to restructure the anti-discrimination work because e-mail, the internet and 24-hour TV have changed the rules of engagement.

A Common European Identity and Islam

This relentless flow of negative information has created a scary atmosphere in Europe, which is being used by some Europeans to argue for a specific identity based on common values. In this artificially manufactured single European identity, there is no space for non-Anglo-Saxon values. In the much-repeated arguments of 'The Clash of Civilisations', it does not matter so much whether ethnic minorities look like the native Europeans, think like them or follow what they believe. The bottom line is that the 'Enemy' has been identified and this enemy is Islam, Muslims and the Islamic World. In the old days, the shouting on the streets was: "Paki, go home" or "Niggers, go to Africa". Today, one often hears: "Muslims, leave our Christian lands", or "Jews, go to Israel".

Very few people in Europe question this simple discourse which is in fact based on present-day media suppositions and also caused by an ignorance of world history. The Western argument is simple: Islamic countries *en masse* have failed to conform to the Western political and economic agenda and thus the map must be redrawn and democracy should be introduced by liberating the poor Muslim masses – by force if necessary. The US's recent campaigns to spread democracy in the Middle East fit very well into this picture.

This line of thinking is successfully advanced by most politicians and the media by exploiting the events of September 11, 2001. This method of reasoning helps scare people, and justifies even more restrictive asylum laws and laws against family reunions, civil liberties and human rights. The EU laws against terrorism and their extremely strict implementation in all EU countries are an extension of such policies. On the surface, these anti-terrorism laws are justified by provoking the name of *Al-Qaeda, Islamism* and *Islamic terrorism*. Yet the end result in this process is that even though every Muslim is perceived as a potential enemy of the State, these laws are also suppress internal dissent, discredit political opponents and abuse the human rights of all citizens. Legal experts and human rights organisations in many countries have expressed reservations about this climate of scare-mongering.

A truly frightening example of the consequences of such policies could be seen at the end of January, 2005. The British Home Minister at that time, Charles Clarke, proposed some drastic anti-terrorism measures in Parliament, measures which gave the authorities the power to put people under unlimited house arrest, impose a curfew on them, deny them the use of telephones and the internet, and also use electronic tagging devices on the bodies of suspected criminals to keep an eye on their movements. On top of this, these measures would have been undertaken on behalf of the Home Secretary and not by court order.

The civil society in the UK reacted sharply against such proposals. The political commentator Peter Hitchens in the newspaper Daily Mail wrote: "Great Britain with its ID cards, removal of civil rights and enormous police powers is turning into a fascist state."[1] Sadly, such negative trends are in direct contradiction to the historical, cultural, social, political and until recently economic traditions of the majority of Europeans, and also to the spirit of a blessed continent with a unique civilisation and democratic roots.

The Future is Bleak

Unfortunately, behind the beautiful democratic face of Europe, there lies a hidden reality which is ugly, racist and inhumane. In fact, some EU leaders are hell-bent on creating a United States of Europe, a White, Christian, economical giant, powerful enough to take on the USA and Japan, as well as other emerging powers like China, India and Brazil, both politically and financially. The Agreement, which was adopted by EU heads of state in Lisbon in October 2007 and signed in December 2007 in Brussels stipulates that EU would have a President, a Foreign Minister and a common EU policy on important issues such as defence, diplomatic corps, intelligence agencies, international treaties and relations. The Chairman of the EU Commission, José Manual Barroso, has called this new EU an empire with a massive economy and which is on its way to becoming a superpower (Press Conference – Strasbourg, 10. 07. 2007).

It is in this powerful EU that nearly 23 million non-European, Third World people (mostly dark-coloured and Muslim) live in poor housing conditions, doing dirty and low-paid jobs, and feeling the arrows of racism everyday. Meanwhile, respected politicians, experts, lawyers, priests and other authorities are busy accusing immigrants and refugees of threatening European culture and social welfare. While talking about human rights in other parts of the world, Europe is busy building new barricades around itself, making a true 'Fortress Europe'. As if that was not enough, the political landscape has also changed dramatically.

Today most of European countries have right-wing governments. This domination was reinforced by ten new member states from Eastern and Central Europe that have very poor records as far as abuses of human rights and racism are concerned.

1 http://hitchensblog.mailonsunday.co.uk [15. 03. 2010].

The poor treatment of the Roma people in these countries is well-documented. With this gloomy future in sight, ethnic minorities and progressive forces are asking themselves:

- What now?
- Would the EU's changing political landscape result in personal and multi-level oppression?
- Does this mean a further tightening of an already very restrictive family reunion and asylum policy in the EU?

The answers are on the immediate horizon. The new Europe is turning towards populism with full force. It appears that this right turn in political circles is not stopping at public debate forums but is also having civil and legal consequences, as described earlier. Since such dire political observations may sound unfair, it can be cross-checked by looking at some data.

Europeans Prefer Immigrants from Other European Countries

Another dire consequence of this non-stop focus on non-European minorities was discovered and measured by an opinion poll carried out by the American Research Centre PEW on June 4, 2003.[2] The survey points towards some very disturbing trends. 67 % of Italians, 60 % of Germans, 50 % of French and 47 % of British people did not want immigration from Africa or the Middle East. When it came to movement from within EU, the feelings were very different. Nearly 60 % of French, German and British people preferred immigrants from neighbouring countries, mostly from Eastern Europe. The Research Centre also compared the situation with what it was twelve years ago and found out that even at that time, hostility was no less than today. In Eastern European countries, the survey found xenophobia and anti-Roma sentiments to be even greater.

According to another opinion poll conducted by Euro-Barometer for the European Commission,[3] 80 % of EU citizens favoured stricter entry restrictions on foreigners from non-EU countries. At the same time, 56 % of Europeans recognised the economic need for immigrants and 34 % did not want to give equal rights to legal immigrants.

2 http://pewresearch.org/topics/immigration [15. 03. 2010].
3 http://www.gesis.org/en/services/data/survey-data/eurobarometer-data-service [15. 03. 2010].

The most recent survey conducted by the World Economic Forum, released in January 2008,[4] and a Gallup Poll published in February 2008[5] point to some very disturbing developments. Nearly 69 % Europeans consider any co-operation with the Muslim world to be a threat to the West. Luckily, the majority of people in the Muslim world actually appreciate democracy and human rights in the West and want the same in their own countries.

The Present Socio-Economic Situation

As a result of minorities being unwelcome in the societies of most EU-countries, unemployment among ethnic and religious minorities is 4 to 5 times higher than the among native peoples, whose unemployment rate is between 6 to 12 %. In my own adopted country, Denmark, unemployment among large ethnic groups is over 50 %. In some groups, such as Somalis, Iraqis, Palestinians and Roma, it is nearly 90 %. Minority women are the hardest hit. Authorities and politicians are aware of the situation, but are afraid to initiate the necessary measures to solve the problem of high unemployment among ethnic minorities. One explanation is that the politicians fear the reactions of their voters. This has led to a situation where the issues of immigration and integration are intentionally included in every election campaign, media debate and even in parliamentary discussions.

I fervently believe that this tactic is a political ploy to avoid the painful restructuring of the labour situation that would allow those ethnic minorities to get a foothold in the labour market. The interesting aspect of the whole immigration debate is that all European countries long ago officially stopped letting migrant workers enter. But still, people who are actually asylum seekers or those who come via family reunions are cynically being presented as immigrants or at worst economical immigrants.

On the social level, many native Europeans are reluctant to have ethnic minorities as their neighbours or co-workers, or have their children go to schools with large percentages of students from ethnic minorities. These minorities are now viewed as a cultural, social and economic menace – a development which has been largely created by the mainstream political establishment through the media, who have fallen upon ethnic minorities as an easy-to-target contemporary scapegoat.

4 http://www.weforum.org/en/events/ArchivedEvents/AnnualMeeting2008/index.htm [15. 03. 2010].

5 http://eu.gallup.com/home.aspx [15. 03. 2010].

Legal Status under Threat

It is true that in time and particularly in order to avoid deportation because of the most minor crimes, a large proportion of ethnic minorities in most EU-countries have obtained citizenship. This has formally given them equal rights with the indigenous citizens, and subsequently equal rights in the EU, i. e. the right to work, to study, to receive medical care and social benefits, and the right to vote. These rights are, on the other hand, not readily available for those who still do not have citizenship of in an EU country. Until very recently, they could not even visit their families in other EU countries without difficulties.

The co-ordination of asylum and immigration policies throughout the EU and the inclusion what was formerly known as the Schengen Agreement into the EU's supranational management is having very restrictive consequences for those ethnic minorities who do not have EU citizenship. In all EU countries, governments are tightening asylum, visa and family reunion laws. Bad practices from one country are quickly copied in other countries under the banner: 'If it is possible in Denmark, why not in Holland?'

Many EU countries are linking citizenship to good behaviour, pledges of loyalty and adoption of the western customs and culture. The French ban on the wearing of religious symbols in schools and government offices is now being debated in most European countries. Some are even considering following suit. An increasing wave of anti-Semitism and Islamophobia is changing the way Europeans perceive Jews and Muslims in their societies. The commissioning and publication of insulting caricatures of the Prophet Mohammed by the newspaper Jyllands-Posten in September 2005 in Denmark and then in other European newspapers, another case of an artist drawing the Prophet as a dog in 2007 in Sweden, the re-publishing of the original Danish caricatures in 17 Danish newspapers in February 2008, the Dutch politician Gert Wilder's anti-Islam film 'Fitna' in March 2008 and many more uncalled for provocations have created deep divisions between Muslim communities and their host societies; moreover, this arrogant demonstration of power on the part of a few individuals has also hurt the relationship between the West and the Islamic world. In this climate of mistrust, one can rightfully ask: Are EU policies especially damaging for ethnic minorities who live here?

Right now, it is difficult to answer this question. Only time will tell. But if history and experience is any key, then there is not much cause for optimism. Most EU-countries have a history of colonialism, which no democratic or civilised society could be proud of today. Most ethnic minorities in the EU come from developing countries, which do not have the political clout to protect their citizens within the EU. For the ethnic minorities, the writing on the wall is clear. It reads: Those of you who want to live here: Be prepared to live as second-class citizens, without equal rights and without equal opportunities, or else pack your bags and leave. And those of you, who are planning to come here: Don't try, stay where you are!

Although there are a huge number of concrete examples available to illustrate the accelerating official trend, here are some examples of the tightening of the rope.

New Restrictive Laws Regarding Aliens

Most countries in the EU – such as Austria, Denmark, Holland, France, Sweden, the UK, Germany and Spain – have passed draconian laws in the last 6 to7 years which require that foreigners not only must learn the native language but sit through tough exams that even local people would be unable to pass. A failure can result in an individual not obtaining permanent residence or, in some countries, that s/he be kicked out of the country. In Danish and Dutch family reunion laws, spouses must learn the language in their own homelands before joining their families.

The situation is even worst in Eastern and Central European countries where large linguistic minorities live. Baltic States like Estonia and Latvia have denied citizenship to many people who could not master the national language because, under Soviet rule, they only spoke Russian. These people have lived all their lives in these countries.

This 'Integration Contract' law is applicable to all foreigners who come to the country now. The laws do not apply to EU citizens, to people who can prove a certain level of language proficiency and to high ranking professionals who have reside in the country less than two years. The law also requires that foreigners entering some of these countries for residence purposes must produce a health certificate and undergo DNA and HIV tests. In Denmark, the government has crossed all lines of civility by demanding that anyone coming in to the country for the sake of work or residence must sign a 'pledge of loyalty' to uphold democratic values.

EU Border Controls

EU asked all ten countries in Eastern and Central Europe who joined the EU in May 2004 to introduce tighter border controls and stop 'illegal immigration'. On July 24, 2002, Poland became the last to sign such an agreement. Poland was asked to hire 5,300 extra border guards by the end of 2006, build ten new border posts and buy new surveillance equipment. Libya, Ukraine and Kenya were asked to establish 'Camps' to hold people deemed illegal immigrants.

On July 19, 2002, the EU Commission asked the European Space Agency to help draw plans to monitor the flow of 'irregular immigrants' with the help of the most modern space satellites, a system called the 'Earth Observation Satellite System'.

The tightening of asylum laws had the desired effects in EU Member States. For example, since the right-wing government came to power in November 2001 in Denmark, it has passed almost 40 laws curtailing the rights of immigrants and refugees. To bring your family to Denmark after marriage, one has to live in Denmark for 24 or 28 years, depending on the fulfilment of certain requirements. It takes eleven years to get citizenship, and in order to get a tourist visa for family members you have to make a deposit of 50,000 Kroners, or nearly 7,000 Euro. The former Integration Minister of Denmark, Mr. Bertel Haarder, opposed the idea of a common integration policy for all EU countries. However, he asserted that the EU should have a common policy on asylum, immigration and the treatment of third country nationals. Yet here, Mr. Haarder would have liked the EU to follow in the footstep of tight Danish laws passed by the Danish Parliament on July 1, 2002.

The number of people asking for asylum from Afghanistan, Iraq and Somalia has fallen drastically. The same trend is taking hold in Holland, the UK and many other EU countries. Besides the drop in asylum seekers, the ratio of those who obtained refugee status in the EU also dropped sharply. For example, in Denmark many more restrictions have been introduced with the result that in 2004, out of nearly 3,000 seekers only 167 persons were given asylum. The same restrictive trend has continued ever since. The former Danish Integration Minister Mr. Haarder even introduced a bill in parliament making it mandatory for social workers in the municipalities to spy on their minority clients and provide information to the immigration department, without the knowledge of the persons concerned. The UK Home Office in 2004 sent a circular that clarified Britain's position on the right of asylum seekers to work. This right has been withdrawn. The reason being given was that asylum cases were being dealt with quickly, mostly within less than a six-month time span.

The EU now wants to go even further to tighten the EU's external borders. According to the Euro Observer in Brussels, on February 13, 2008 EU home Affairs Commissioner Franco Frattini tabled a border control package consisting of three proposals:

1. Setting up an entry/exit register of non-European visitors to the EU.
2. A European Border Surveillance System designed to detect those who enter the bloc between border crossing points.
3. Better use of the EU's border control agency, Frontex, particularly via 'intensified' joint operations between member states at sea borders.

The above-mentioned examples provide a taste of what is coming in the future.

What Is the EU Doing to Stop Racism?

When it comes to fighting racism, we have to look at two different approaches: first at the official response and then at NGO activities. In the past, key dates have marked the EU's genuine political commitment to combat racism and xenophobia and highlighted the dynamic development of a coherent EU policy on these key issues.

- In 1995, the Commission published a communiqué on racism, xenophobia and anti-Semitism.
- In 1996, the institutions adopted a joint action to combat racism and xenophobia.
- In 1997, the EU Monitoring Centre on Xenophobia and Racism (EUMC) was established following the European Year Against Racism.
- In 1998, the action plan against racism was adopted.
- In 1999, at the Tampere Summit, the European Council called "for the fight against racism and xenophobia to be stepped up."[6]
- In 2000, two equality directives were adopted to fight discrimination.
- In 2001, a framework decision on combating racism and xenophobia was proposed, tackling the issue of racism as a crime. The same year, member states declared at the Laeken Summit that "racism is on the rise".[7] Although the directives were not fully implemented, member states moved to put in place measures that would give protection to ethnic and religious minorities.
- In April 2007, the EU Council of Ministers approved in principle that racism should be treated as a crime.
- 2007 was the European Year for Equal Opportunities For All. Many consultation processes took place on national levels and on the EU level.
- 2008 is the Year for Intercultural Dialogue. It is designed to bring various population groups together so that they can learn about each other.
- The European Union has a Social Inclusion agenda to address the needs of ethnic and religious minorities.

6 *European Commission*: Tampere European Council, 15-16 October 1999. Presidency Conclusions; http://www.consilium.europa.eu/ueDocs/cms_Data/docs/pressData/en/ec/00200-r1.en9.htm [15. 03. 2010].

7 *European Commission*: Laeken European Council, 14-15 December 2001. Presidency Conclusions; http://www.consilium.europa.eu/ueDocs/cms_Data/docs/pressData/en/ec/68827.pdf [15. 03. 2010].

- The EU Commission is also preparing to introduce a new anti-discrimination directive outside the labour market.

On the surface, all these efforts should have made a significant dent in the wall of racism. The EU institutions, especially, the Commission has tried to persuade national governments not only to abide by the directives it has issued, but also use the maximum standards to implement them. Many governments have tried to congratulate themselves on the job well done. At ENAR, the European Network Against Racism, we believe that many EU countries have abdicated their responsibilities in the fight against racism – and ENAR is worried about this course of action. ENAR's yearly reports since 2004 have given a clear picture of the increasing socio-economic hardship inflicted on ethnic and religious minorities from non-European countries within the EU.

Despite the strong promises made by all governments in 2000 to establish minimum standards to protect every person residing on European territory against the forms of discrimination listed in Article 13, the slow transposition of these instruments eight years later shows that a lot still needs to be done. Implementing a coherent European anti-discrimination policy is indeed a long-term project that will need permanent corrective mechanisms to address in depth the root causes of prejudice and exclusion and ultimately create a Europe where everyone enjoys equal rights. The situation is so acute that the European Commission has taken legal steps against many member states by suing them in the Court of Justice. These states have failed to adopt two key EU anti-discrimination laws.

According to a Commission spokeswoman, the backlog in implementation in some member states means "people in these countries still miss the protection by European law, for example if they are treated unfavourably because of their race. National anti-discrimination legislation offers no alternative to these EU citizens. The countries lagging behind in the transposition of EU law are exactly those where national legislation is insufficient."[8] A few countries have even breached EU law by failing to fully transpose the directive prohibiting discrimination on the grounds of race or ethnicity by July 19, 2003 deadline, though this is not true of any of the 10 new Member States, who had to ensure that their legislation complied with the directives by the time of their accession to the EU on May 1, 2004. The main reason that many countries do not implement the directives in letter and spirit could be the lack of sanctions. There are no practical consequences with which the Commission can threaten these countries. There are no sanctions in place like the ones the EU used against Austria, which forced the member state to change its practices and respect the directives issued.

8 http://ec.europa.eu/index_en.htm [15. 03. 2010].

The reality is that very little has been done to check the rise of racism from 2001 to 2004. Since 2004, one does notice a slow movement in the positive direction by both EU institutions and also by other actors in the field. For example:

- Public consultation on a non-discrimination green paper covering the new enlarged EU has begun. This paper, issued in June 2004, took stock of EU anti-discrimination activities and possible ways to reinforce these efforts. The paper also disclosed that majority of people asked stated that the EU anti-discrimination legislation has so far had limited or no impact in preventing racism.
- There was a European Stop Discrimination Truck Tour from September 2004 to April 2007.
- The Council of Europe's Commission against racism (ECRI) issued policy recommendations against anti-Semitism in October 2004.
- The EU Parliament established an Anti-Racism and Diversity Group in November 2004 with ENAR's help.
- The EU Constitution was signed in Rome on October 29, 2004, reinforcing fundamental rights and non-discrimination in the EU, but the whole project was scrapped because France and Holland voted no in their referenda. In its stead, a new treaty known as the Lisbon Agreement is now in place.
- In 2004, the OSCE held three conferences on issues of anti-Semitism and racism in Berlin, Paris and Brussels. NGOs were asked to give their input.
- In March 2004, UNESCO launched an initiative to establish an inter-city network with a ten-point plan to combat racism.
- In 2004, eleven Common Basic Principles on Integration were adopted by the European Council.

On the other hand, in December 2004, under the presidency of Holland, the EU adopted the Hague Programme which replaced the 1999 Tampere decisions. Unfortunately, anti-discrimination and anti-racism were not specifically mentioned in this programme. So we were back to the drawing board again.

Since 2004, there have been many developments in the broad agenda of migration policy, including the proposed directive on common standards and procedures in member states for returning third country nationals residing illegally within the EU and the proposed EU directive providing for sanctions against employers of irregular third country nationals; yet many of these developments have the potential to undermine the basic human rights of third country nationals. While the framework directive on the basic socio-economic rights for all third country workers aims to fill the rights gap, there are concerns that the priority given to immigration control in bringing forward proposals on regular and irregular migration distorts the framework.

Anti-discrimination is being replaced by new terminology such as integration, inter-culturalism, social inclusion, diversity and political human rights. I am a great supporter of human rights, but they should be both political and socio-economic. The march of human rights should not be a 'Trojan Horse' used by neo-liberals to stifle the question of anti-racism.

Efforts to Secure Race Equality in Eastern European Countries

On July 19, 2005, which was the fifth anniversary of the official publication of the EU Race Directive, the European Roma Rights Centre (ERRC) submitted detailed comments on the measures taken to date in five European countries to implement the principle of equal treatment, irrespective of racial or ethnic origin. Speaking on the occasion of the anniversary of this directive, ERRC Acting Executive Director Claude Cahn said:

> "Czech parliamentarians have sabotaged efforts to approve a comprehensive anti-discrimination law. The Polish government has not yet seriously even tried to adopt one. In Hungary, Romania and Slovakia, positive moves by the legislature have been followed by inertia, incompetence or obstruction by implementing authorities. New laws in those countries have not yet made even the shallowest dent in a reality of pervasive racial exclusion because the administration has yet to implement them well, where it has tried to implement these laws at all. These failures mean little change on the ground for several million Roma – the group most affected by the forces of racial hatred in Central and Eastern Europe today."[9]

From the EUMC to the EU Fundamental Rights Agency

The European Monitoring Centre was one of the major products of the 1997 European Year Against Racism. It enhanced the visibility of Europe's commitment and produced valuable research and recommendations for the development of both EU and national policies in the fight against racism and xenophobia. However, the Council unexpectedly decided in December 2003 to broaden the mandate of the EUMC to transform it into a Fundamental Rights Agency. Unfortunately this useful monitoring centre is now being reorganised. There is nothing wrong with focusing on human rights, but human rights can and should go hand in hand with anti-racism and anti-discrimination efforts.

---

9 *European Roma Rights Centre*: 5th Birthday EU Race Directive: Central Europe Does Not Comply, 19. 07. 2005; http://www.errc.org/cikk.php?cikk=2283 [15. 03. 2010].

By changing the focus of the EUMC, the issue of anti-racism has once again been marginalised. Safeguards need to be given to preserve the resources, focus and visibility of the centre's actions against racism. According to Amnesty International, the new body should fill the gap between principle and practice that exists in the EU's addressing of human rights within its own borders. However, the organisation doubted its real impact and suggested that it is likely to have a marginal role, as member states will not allow it "to exercise any real oversight of the respect for human rights in their own countries."[10]

Governments and the General Public Should Be More Aware of Racism

Civil society continues to draw the attention of the general public and governments to the fact that racism is on the rise. Racist and xenophobic crimes continue to be reported daily. In fact, political parties openly developing a political programme based on racist and xenophobic propaganda have even become members of a number of governments in Europe. These right-wing political parties are co-operating with one another across the EU. In December 2004, the UK newspaper The Guardian reported that the Belgian politician and leader of the Vlaams Belang Party, Filip De Winter, had asked Austrian politician Jörg Haider to lead a united front of anti-immigrant European parties such as Austria's Freedom Party, France's National Front, the Liga Nord from Italy and the Dutch New Right Party. De Winter also said that the purpose of this coalition would be to fight the "Islamisation of Europe."[11] Paradoxically, this evidence was totally ignored by European decision-makers who, since the 2001 Laeken Declaration, have steadily marginalised any EU action against racism on their political agenda by no longer condemning racism in the presidency conclusions of the European Council. Discussions within the Convention about the future of this issue and about the EU's competence in combating racism and xenophobia within the realms of justice and home affairs have been extremely difficult.

The assessment of the prevailing political situation makes it clear that the time has come for the EU to put words into action and remember the forgotten commitments of the past. Time and again, ENAR has called upon the different EU presidencies and all EU member states to fulfil their obligations at last and work towards a Europe free from racism.

10 http://asiapacific.amnesty.org/library/Index/ENGIOR610032005?open&of=ENG-312 [15. 03. 2010].

11 *Traynor, Ian*: Europe's Far-Right Parties Hold Coalition Talks, in: The Guardian Online, 10. 12. 2004; http://www.guardian.co.uk/world/2004/dec/10/thefarright.politics [15. 03. 2010].

The Ethnic Minority Response

The challenge of self-organisation has been staring us in the face for a long time. That is why it is important for minority communities to be organised so that they can ask that their basic human rights be protected in the countries where they live. The EU must also be reminded that violations of human rights occur in Europe on a daily basis.

Only on the basis of actual and reasonable information will it be possible for ethnic minorities to fight for their right to equal opportunity and to a decent life in Europe. It is necessary for the various ethnic organisations in Europe to enter into a constructive and forward-looking dialogue with each other and with the progressive forces in different European countries. Since the most effective campaign would be a united reaction from minorities across Europe, NGOs did take action in 1998 and established the largest anti-racist network in Europe: ENAR, the European Network against Racism. ENAR consists of over 650 anti-racist NGOs from all EU countries. It was established to raise the issue of racism specifically – and not those of diversity or integration or even multi-culturalism, but rather racial discrimination – and to lobby EU institutions. ENAR believes that the EU has deserted the anti-racism battlefield. Evidence of such a disregard for anti-racism is unquestionable. During the 2003 Convention negotiations on the future of Europe, it was extremely difficult to maintain the EU's competence in combating racism and xenophobia within the domains of justice and home affairs.

ENAR has been successful in alerting the public – both European and International – of the dangers of this accelerating negative trend. The international media (printed press, TV and radio) have not only used ENAR as a source of information but also sought its opinion and comments on the issues of discrimination, racism, different EU initiatives, immigration and the changing political landscapes in Europe. Journalists from publications as diverse as The Mainichi Times (Japan), Time Magazine, The Economist, The Washington Post, The Daily Telegraph, The Guardian, Le Monde, El Mondo, de Volkskrant (Holland) to TV Channels such as BBC World Service, ABC (USA), the German national TV station ARD, Swedish TV, CNN and many more have interviewed ENAR's representatives.

The international community has taken notice and begun to raised its voice. That is where anti-racist and humanist groups should increasingly set their focus if they wish to stop the march of the right. As mentioned before, we have also established a group on anti-racism and diversity within the EU Parliament, which will help to lobby politicians in the EU and in individual countries. But all these actions are a mere drop in the ocean. We need a true people's movement. Ethnic minorities and the progressive forces of anti-racism must join hands. This co-operation must be above party politics, political ideologies and devoid of any patronising arrogance. We must work to build up Europe, a new Europe without prejudices, bubbling with a deeply-felt openness. Europe can create peace and welfare for all; it can be a place where ethnic minorities are not only tolerated but also respected as fellow human beings. Racism not only hurts minorities but also eats the soul of the majority. It is like a boomerang. Sooner or later, it is going to hit all of us in the face.

A Word of Advice to Ethnic Minority Organisations

There are many active grassroots organisations fighting racism. They must realise that it is perhaps time to change their campaign tactics. Until now, all their efforts and focus have been to inform the European public and the authorities in the hope that minorities will be accepted as equal citizens, as resources instead of burdens. In doing so, minority NGOs and representatives have quite possibly unintentionally neglected the most important factor in the struggle, namely the ethnic minorities themselves, i. e. the men and women on the street who bear the brunt of discrimination, who have nowhere to turn to and whose voice nobody hears. Today we must focus on these people.

In the past, there have been many meetings and conferences within Europe to discuss these issues, such as EC in 1992, an European anti-discrimination directive campaign, an open border campaign, an anti-racist youth campaign, Starting Line, and many more. I believe that the biggest responsibility of ethnic minority organisations in each country today is to inform their own members about their legal rights and the political situation in both the countries they live in and in Europe as a whole. In order to survive as marginalised group or as an individual in a society where power structures are very established, it is necessary to maintain one's self respect, cultural roots and family ties.

Practical Steps

Strategies for a Europe-wide campaign should be worked out both on national and pan-European levels. On a national level, one can work with educational institutions, solidarity organisations, human rights organisations and sympathetic European MPs. Minorities should obtain written pledges of support from MPs and MEPs. Minority communities must be fully aware of their voting rights in order for them to wield political leverage. Local public opinion can also be mobilised through media and political lobbying. Lately a lot of work has been done on the race relations issue within the EU, but sadly there is no united political voice to speak fearlessly for the rights of black and ethnic minorities in individual EU countries. It would be nice if NGOs could rise to the challenge and provide an alternative political platform. Through real and detailed information, it would be possible for minorities to fight for their equal rights and to have a higher quality life in Europe. An effective campaign must be well-coordinated. Unless ethnic minorities themselves raise the question of discrimination, very little will be done. By creating a common front, minorities will be able to gain the influence they need. It is important for these organisations to start a constructive international dialogue with each other.

Political Goals

In order to achieve specific political goals, a permanent secretariat could be established wherein active grassroots anti-racist and ethnic minority organisations from different countries can pool their resources and information, exchange experiences, give out literature, and also contact the media and politicians. This council is not meant to replace present networks like ENAR but to support their work by mobilisation the minority groups themselves. Most ethnic minorities are already engaged on the local and national level. They know the issues, the people, the problems and also the possible solutions. All they need now is unity, focus, discipline and co-operation across ethnic, national and religious lines. If they want to survive in Europe, not as a single entity but as part of the entire system, they must be united.

In order to influence a political system, one must first understand how it works, which can only be learned through experience. Therefore minorities must demand the right to be represented by themselves and not by surrogates. This wish can be transmitted publicly through the media and through the political system. But I would like to raise a word of caution here. Influence will not be served up on a silver platter; it has to be gained through political struggle and based on clear analysis and the doing away with wishful thinking, and as well as on close cooperation with those Europeans who still believe in human rights, pluralistic development and most of all in keeping their societies democratic.

A Successful Anti-Racist Struggle Can Be Achieved through the Following:

- The exchange of experiences with countries who have years of experience of multi-cultural, multi-ethnic and multi-religious work.
- Close contact with ethnic minority organisations, minority politicians, religious leaders, leading business people, neutral researchers, solidarity organisations and NGOs.
- When making laws and decisions, one must keep international human rights conventions and democratic principles of equality in mind.
- Strong legal protection for minorities must be available, for example via a kind of anti-discrimination ombudsman.
- Affirmative action to advance involvement in the labour market.
- Being open to change and not saying, "That is not the way we do things."

- Positive political signals are important for psychological security of minorities.
- The principle of ethnic equality must be incorporated in every initiative.
- Focusing on diversity instead of uniformity – in education and in cultural and social life. However, it must be done with deep respect to the norms of the people.
- Decisions must not be imposed but explained.

The late great American writer Susan Sontag once said:

> "Some people claim that Europe is dead. Maybe it will be right to say that Europe is yet to be born. A Europe that takes care of its defenceless minorities is badly needed. It is necessary that Europe be multi-cultural, otherwise it will cease to exist."

Only fools would argue against that.

References

Castles, Stephen/Davidson, Alastair: Citizenship and Migration. Globalization and the Politics of Belonging, New York 2000

European Commission: Laeken European Council, 14-15 December 2001. Presidency Conclusions; http://www.consilium.europa.eu/ueDocs/cms_Data/docs/pressData/en/ec/68827.pdf [15. 03. 2010]

European Commission: Tampere European Council, 15-16 October 1999. Presidency Conclusions; http://www.consilium.europa.eu/ueDocs/cms_Data/docs/pressData/en/ec/00200-r1.en9.htm [15. 03. 2010]

European Network Against Racism: ENAR Shadow Reports. 2004, 2005 and 2006; http://www.enar-eu.org/Page.asp?docid=19048&langue=EN [15. 03. 2010]

European Network Against Racism: For a Real European Citizenship, Brussels 2001

European Roma Rights Centre: 5th Birthday EU Race Directive: Central Europe Does Not Comply, 19. 07. 2005; http://www.errc.org/cikk.php?cikk=2283 [15. 03. 2010]

Huntington, Samuel P.: The Clash of Civilisations? in: Foreign Affairs, No. 3, Vol. 72, 1993

Niessen, Jan/Schibel, Yongmi: Demographic Changes and the Consequences for Europe's Future. Is Immigration an Option?, Brussels 2002

Quaker Council for European Affairs: Around Europe, No. 251, Brussels 2003

Quraishy, Bashy: Ethnic Minorities in the West. Conflict or Enrichment, 1995

Quraishy Bashy: Searching for a Humane Europe. Ethnic Minorities in the European Union, 1998

Scagliotti, Luciano: Raum der Freiheit, der Sicherheit und des Rechts: Einwanderung und Asyl – eine kurze Aktualisierung. Paper Presented at the PSE-Conference 'Area of Freedom, Security and Justice: Four Years after Tampere – Our Proposals for the Future', 13-14 October 2003 in Tampere, Finland

Traynor, Ian: Europe's Far-Right Parties Hold Coalition Talks, in: The Guardian Online, 10. 12. 2004; http://www.guardian.co.uk/world/2004/dec/10/thefarright.politics [15. 03. 2010]

http://asiapacific.amnesty.org/library/Index/ENGIOR610032005?open&of=ENG-312 [15. 03. 2010]

http://ec.europa.eu/index_en.htm [15. 03. 2010]

http://eu.gallup.com/home.aspx [15. 03. 2010]

http://www.gesis.org/en/services/data/survey-data/eurobarometer-data-service [15. 03. 2010]

http://hitchensblog.mailonsunday.co.uk [15. 03. 2010]

http://pewresearch.org/topics/immigration/ [15. 03. 2010]

http://www.weforum.org/en/events/ArchivedEvents/AnnualMeeting2008/index.htm [15. 03. 2010]

Relevant Web Sites in the Context of Work against Racism

http://www.enar-eu.org

http://www.parliament.gov.uk

http://www.migpolgroup.com

http://www.minorityrights.org

http://www.ecre.org

http://www.errc.org

Fostering a 'Religion': Another Side of Multiculturalism[1]

Shigeko Kubota

Introduction

The term multiculturalism[2] is a concept that is still in the process of development, therefore the meaning of the term also varies with its usage. In general, multiculturalism refers to the following, that is, to the coexistence of several cultures in a region, a state or a community, and/or policies and ideological stances that promote the above. Multicultural conditions are not a recent phenomenon, but rather a phenomenon that is common to all ages and regions, in the sense that at present there is no region that is not multicultural. However, the ideology or thought of multiculturalism was born of historical conditions.

With the increase in immigrants from outside Europe, such as Muslims, Europe is experiencing a struggle between the two self-identities of the values of secularised Christianity and the values of intercultural coexistence. These two are perceived as proof of the modernity and progress that Europe has achieved.[3] From the perspective of attitudes toward different cultures, the former is assimilation whereas the latter is multiculturalism. In general, multiculturalism is considered to be superior to assimilation, therefore, in a country like Switzerland, for example, where immigrants are not treated as citizens that are provided for in all aspects but rather as social or economic citizens in the form of producers, consumers, social insurance holders, and taxpayers,[4] the pose of multiculturalism merely serves as a kind of unofficial societal hospitality granted to immigrants in exchange for the inaction of official governmental policies which would actually grant them the rights of full equality under the rule of law.

---

1 This study was made possible by a grant from the Centre for New European Research, Hitotsubashi University, in 2006.

2 It is said that the term 'multiculturalism' first appeared in the 1960s, but Canada was the first that actually implemented it in the form of policies. Since then, this term has been used not only to mean policies but also used to express multicultural conditions and to acknowledge the positive effects of it.

3 *Casanova, José*: Einwanderung und der neue religiöse Pluralismus, pp. 188-191, in: Leviathan. Berliner Zeitschrift für Sozialwissenschaft, No. 2, Vol. 34, 2006, pp. 182-207. According to Casanova, the secularisation of Christianity is closely connected to the self-perception of "normal", "progressive", and "aufgeklärte" (enlightened) Europe. However, on the other hand, multiculturalism is also a proof of the progress of Europe's modernity, which is liberal, democratic and which respects human rights.

4 See *Claudio Bolzman* et al.: La population âgée immigrée face à la retraite. Problème social et problématiques de recherche, in: *Hans-Rudolf Wicker* (ed.): Das Fremde in der Gesellschaft. Migration, Ethnizität und Staat/L'altérité dans la société: migration, ethnicité, État, Zürich 1996, pp. 123-142.

However, this does not necessarily mean that this brings immigrants and their host society any closer together.[5] In the Netherlands, the rights of Muslims are respected, for example, as timeslots for Muslim programs are secured in public broadcasting, Muslims are inspired to awaken to their identity through means other than the measures implemented by the state. The reason for this is said to be because the immigrants feel certain contradictions in various scenes of daily life between the religious and humanistic views of Europe, "which are based on a value system that emphasises the individual rather than the community, such as the family or society, and a social value system based on rationality that respects man-made norms rather than those stipulated by God – values and norms common to Western society in a wider context."[6] In other words, there is opposition to being subsumed by the ideas created by Modern Europe. Racism still exists in Switzerland, and in the Netherlands problems that occur in daily life are not reflected in actual policies, and thus the respect for multiculturalism that is thought to be something positive for immigrants is not necessarily the fundamental solution to the problem. If this is the case, then should we make adjustments or alterations to multiculturalism? Or should we further refine the concept and then apply it to the real world?

Multiculturalism in the U.S. developed in response to social movements that include both opposition from minorities, including immigrants, and changes in their self-perception, whereas multiculturalism in Europe resulted more or less from a campaign, a policy from the top for measures to promote an understanding toward different cultures and religions, which include issues such as whether to accept values that are incompatible with secularised Christianity, how to coexist, where to draw the line between Europe and the outside, all of which are issues that include problems of civilisation. In other words, in Europe multiculturalism was not in response to a movement by minorities, but was the majority's logic behind the integration of immigrants. However, multiculturalism and assimilation are considered to be at opposite ends of the spectrum both in the US and Europe. There is a negative connotation associated with assimilation whereas there is a peculiar sense of optimism with regards to multiculturalism. Around the discourse of multiculturalism, there is a sense that even though the methods are still incomplete, if one con-

5 In March 2007, the U.N. Committee on the Elimination of Racial Discrimination (CERD) submitted a final report to the U.N. Commission on Human Rights concerning the situation of immigrants in Switzerland. In an interview with a member of the press who asked the question, "Die Schweiz ist doch sehr stolz auf ihren Multikulturalismus. Ist das nur ein neuer Mythos, der nun zerbröckelt?" ("Switzerland is very proud of its multiculturalism, but is it not simply a myth?") the Committee replied, "Der Multikulturalismus der Schweiz ist kein Mythos. Wie im Bericht erwähnt, ist er ein Trumpf der Schweizer Gesellschaft" ("As stated in the report, it is not a myth but their best hand"). Cf. Swissinfo, 23. 03. 2007, Tages-Anzeiger 23. 03. 2007.

6 *Masanori, Naito*: Challenge to the West? Awakening of Muslims Immigrants in Western European Countries at the UNU-UNESCO International Conference on the Dialogue of Civilizations, Tokyo 2001.

tinues on with multiculturalism it will lead to a bright future where different cultures and religions will understand one another. However, this optimism seems unstable and is not very convincing in the eyes of someone who has come into contact with many immigrants during field work and who grew up and acquired intellectual training in a culture outside of Europe. Perhaps there is something in common between the instability that an outsider feels and the fact the policies of multiculturalism have not had the expected effects, even though multiculturalism has been enforced and publicity activities have been conducted to emphasise its importance.

The discussion of multiculturalism consists of what form it should take and how it should be promoted. In other words, the question asked is 'in what ways' should multiculturalism be promoted? However, it is necessary to consider the epistemic problems that are intrinsic to multiculturalism as an ideology, especially when considering why multiculturalism, contrary to expectations, has not necessarily been a good thing for immigrants. In this paper, I will try to examine the relations between the two ideas that are thought to be at the two opposite ends of the spectrum by focusing on 'what' rather than 'in what ways'. In the next section, I will consider the discourse that welcomes religious pluralism, which contains issues that overlap with multiculturalism.

Many Religions Do Not Harm Society

On 29 January 2005, an article appeared in the *Neue Zürcher Zeitung* entitled, '*Viele Religionen schaden der Gesellschaft nicht. Von den Gefahren und Chancen der Religionspluralität*'.[7] The following is a summary of the article.

In Zurich religious statistics published in 2004, it was reported that there were 370 churches, religious groups, and centers in that stronghold of Protestantism. What stands out especially is the pluralism within Christianity itself. However, religions other than Christianity have also increased in number. This is a common phenomenon both in Switzerland and in Western Europe. Foreign religions do not stand out and are not as visible as the steeples of churches, but have been pushed into smaller chambers. The following questions may arise: How many religions can stand to exist in one society or city? Would numerous religions harm the stability of society? However, it is surprising to find out that many people think that religion has such powers. Only 30 years ago, religion was thought to be powerless and unmodern. With the appearance of Islam, people have attached exaggerated importance to religion.

7 'Many Religions Do Not Harm Society – Crisis and the Chance of Religious Plurality'; *Baumann, Martin*: Viele Religionen schaden der Gesellschaft nicht. Von den Gefahren und Chancen der Religionspluralität, in: Neue Zürcher Zeitung, 29. 01. 2005.

The author provided the following example from the period before the late 4th century when Christianity became the religion of the Roman Empire, i.e. from the period of Hellenism, to demonstrate that there is no real historical evidence that religious plurality threatens the unity of society but rather that the unilateral dominance of Christianity is an exception. Many cults and religious groups existed at that time. Many gods existed under polytheism, people worshipped different gods according to their circumstances and at the same time it was not strange to belong to several religious groups. In time, however, religious groups started to eliminate each other, and the idea that one follower should not belong to several religions appeared. Moreover, the author looked at examples outside of Europe. He illustrated that both historically and in the present day many religions have simultaneously existed in Asia, and provided examples from India and China. The author stated that in the Chinese cultural sphere, ever since the middle of the 1st century, Confucianism, Taoism and Buddhism have existed at the same time, which could be regarded as religious pluralism, and moreover, that religions were able to coexist without the danger of syncretism, and also that the coexistence of multiple religions is a historical phenomenon in many cultural spheres.

In the latter half of the article, the author pointed out that the present day situation in Europe wherein many religions coexist was accelerated by the flow of immigrants, that the threat people felt due to the existence of multiple religions was especially heightened on account of the various problems that had surfaced relating to Muslims, and that this new religious pluralism (*der neue Religionspluralismus*) not only contains problems but can provide new opportunities and benefits.

There are two problems in this article. One is that even though the author uses the word religion in general (and in other parts he uses the word *Lehre*, or doctrine), he applies the specific religious concept of Christianity to the situation in 1st century China and stated that it was possible for three religions to coexist in that period. Secondly, it is questionable whether the examples from Hellenism, India and China are appropriate examples to demonstrate that the 'new religious pluralism' accelerated by immigrants, the topic of this article, will not become a threat to society.

The Concept of Religion

As a Japanese person, I cannot help but feel a sense of peculiarity to see Confucianism, Taoism and Buddhism be provided as an example of religious coexistence, because none of the three seem to fit the concept of 'religion'. Buddhism and Shinto in Japan are also referred to as religions, however the word 'religion' was imported from Europe,[8] and such a concept is not indigenous to Japan. The way in which the Japanese relate to Buddhism or Shinto is different to the way people in Europe relate to Christianity. There are certain aspects that cannot be expressed by the word religion. For example, many people in Japan have difficulty answering the question "what is your religion?" That is not to say that Japanese are 'atheists'. It is simply extremely difficult to express the aspects of our spiritual activities by using the Japanese translation of the word 'religion' derived from the West. What is called Buddhism or Shinto is different from the notion of religion that is based on Christianity. In China, the word 'religion' has also been imported from Europe. Moreover, it was not imported directly, but rather China imported the Japanese translation. Of course, it is difficult to explain Chinese culture via the word 'religion'. It is especially difficult to explain Confucianism as religion, because Confucianism is a system of ethics that regulated the relationship and actions between the superior and subordinate classes. Taoism and Buddhism cannot be discussed on an equal plane, nor can they be explained by the concept of religion. Therefore, it is erroneous to consider that the situation in China is the same as the present-day situation of religious coexistence in Europe. This is not only because there is a difference in the concept of religion but also because there is a difference in the perception of what religion ought to be in society.

Although separate from the issue of semantics, it is possible to observe the difference in the perception of religion between immigrants and their host societies in present-day Europe. For example, there is a community of Tibetans in exile in Switzerland. In the Tibetan language, the word that corresponds to religion is 'chos'. 'Chos' is the order of the universe (Shinra Bansho) and the order of human society. Therefore, it is related to all aspects of life including academics, politics, medicine and one's general way of life. At present, not all immigrants live with this kind of idea. However, their 'religious scene' greatly differs from the practice of those Swiss who have an interest in Tibetan Buddhism. The religious rituals con-

8 Japan's policy of isolation started in 1639 ended 220 years later in 1858. Since then, Western culture has entered and penetrated into Japan in a very short span of time. The word religion was imported from Europe around this time and translated into Japanese. While the West did exert a great cultural influence on the non-West (including Japan) during the modernization process, this of course does not mean that the thoughts and ideas at the local level have been completely overturned or that there has been a dialectical integration of the two. It can be said that both coexist in parallel. In Japan, not only religion, but words such as society and individual were translated and China, who uses the same characters as the Japanese, imported many of them. In Europe, these concepts may be immediately obvious, but they did not exist in Japan or China, or if they did exist it was in a completely different form.

ducted by Tibetans are very simple. Monks from India who are stationed in Switzerland attend various events such as the Dalai Lama's birthday, Constitution Day and meetings of the women's association, and recite the Sutra. Many may think that the religious conduct at such a gathering is filled with a 'religious' atmosphere in complete silence, similar to mass at a Christian church, but that is not always the case. In fact, there is an almost chaotic atmosphere as some small children run around and people take pictures. This kind of atmosphere is similar to the service conducted in Tibetan temples in India. Sometimes a Ringpoche (a high-ranking monk) from India visits the temples in Switzerland, and preaches all day long. However, he does not speak in a manner to grab the short attention span of the people, but rather continues to speak about difficult issues that are hard for the lay public to understand. During the preaching, some close their eyes and meditate, and some even drink tea. Some even have mentioned that the significance lies in listening to the voice and being in the same space as the Ringpoche rather than in trying to understand the content of his speech.

On the other hand, in the Buddhist centers that Swiss people go to, one can witness various forms of practice, from centres that conduct worship just like at a Christian mass, where a Sutra translated into German is sung like a hymn, to those that focus most of their time on meditation. However, at these kinds of centres, what is important is the understanding of Buddhist ideas and thoughts and the 'religious' atmosphere. According to Daniel Valentine,[9] the important thing for 'religion' understood in the Christian context is not *is-ness* (what something is) but *about-ness* (what something is about), not ontology but epistemology, not mood but mind, and – if I may be allowed to add something to this – not body but understanding. It is true that meditation emphasizes body rather than understanding, but it seems as if there is a difference in whether the objective is the body or not.

9 *Valentine, Daniel E.*: The Arrogation of Being by The Blind-Spot of Religion, in: Hitotsubashi Journal of Social Studies, No. 1, Vol. 33, 2001, pp. 83-102.Valentine talks about the connection between Christianity and faith. He states that the Hindi Sri Lankans that immigrated to the U.S. based their Hindu rituals on Christian concepts; therefore the rituals in the US differ from the rituals seen in Sri Lanka. He refers to this as epistemology and about-ness. This is similar to the difference in the Swiss people's conception and the Tibetan people's conception of Tibetan Buddhism. The reason why Valentine refers to this as about-ness is because he thinks that the characteristic of religion is faith. However, it cannot be clearly stated whether Christianity is linked to faith in present-day Europe. Casanova states that under the social conditions wherein there is an increase in Muslims, the relations between the secularisation of Christianity and the Christian identity is becoming more and more complex in Europe. Casanova also states that although secularisation is "believing without belonging" (Grace Davie), in contemporary society what stands out is "belonging without believing" (Danièle Hervieu-Léger) (*Casanova* 2006, pp. 187). Here, what is referred to as about-ness in how the Swiss relate to Buddhism is being juxtaposed to that of Tibetan Buddhism. However, as indicated by Valentine, it seems as though one can only determine whether the Swiss consider Tibetan Buddhism to be faith on a case-by-case basis.

There is hardly any exchange between the Tibetans and the Swiss that go to the Buddhist centres. The reasons for this include the maintenance of their distinct community as immigrants, and the relations between immigrant identity and religion. However, one must also take into account the difference in the perception of religion between the Tibetans and other Western Buddhists. At the beginning of this paper, I provided an example of how Muslims in the Netherlands, despite the multicultural policies there, cannot help but feel that they cannot adapt to European views on humanism and religion in various aspects of their daily lives. For the Tibetans, with the application of concepts such as 'religion' or 'Tibetan Buddhism', they are being subsumed under European religious views. Some Tibetans have often said that they do not think that the Buddhism practiced in the Buddhist centres that Swiss people attend is the same as Tibetan Buddhism.

Considering Religion

Let us focus on the problem of considering religious coexistence in the early Roman Age, the Age of Hellenism, and in India and China as something similar to the multireligious situation in present-day Europe. The issue concerns the existence of immigrants. Although the same term 'multireligious' is used, the present problem lies not with religion itself but with those who are in charge of it (immigrants). If this article states that the pluralism within Christianity does not threaten society, or that the coexistence of European Buddhists, excluding immigrants as mentioned above, and Christians does not threaten society, then it does relate this to the multireligious situation in the early Roman Age, the Age of Hellenism, or in India and China, in a sense that there was religious pluralism among peoples in the same cultural sphere. Moreover, there may be some points in common between the early Roman Age and contemporary India.[10] The author may have chosen examples from different historical time periods and geographical locales because the concept of religious pluralism used by him was not limited to immigrants, but rather expanded to a wider context to include the diversity within Christianity. However, if that is the case then these examples are even more inappropriate.

The discussion concerning religious pluralism in the present day includes issues relating not only to the religions of immigrants, but to various other issues including the pluralism of Christianity. Christianity, Islam and Tibetan Buddhism as practiced by both Tibetans and the Swiss are all considered to be equal, and this is considered to be religious diversity. This is reflected in actual activities. For example, 'Religious Diversity in the Canton of Lucerne' ('*Religionsviefalt im Kanton Luzern*'), 'Religion in Switzerland' ('*Religionen in der Schweiz*'), 'Inforel' ('*Information Religion*'), and 'Remid' ('*Religionswissenschaftlicher Medien- und Informationsdienst*') all conduct various public relations activities. Moreover, the city of

10 *Valentine* 2001, pp. 28-40, p. 85.

Bern recently bought a piece of unused land and is in the midst of building the 'House of Religion, Dialogue of Cultures' ('*Haus der Religionen, Dialog der Kulturen*'). Through the internet and various events, these institutions promote not only diversity but also the possibility of dialogue and exchange, and highlight the fact that not only traditional Christianity but also various other religions coexist in their towns.

The 'Religious Information in Zurich' report published in 2004 noted that there are 370 religious institutions and groups in the city.[11] These institutions and groups are classified under each religion with its description, and the publication is in dictionary form. Inforel published a similar publication about the 400 religious institutions and groups in the city of Basel. There are a number of publications similar to these religion dictionaries. For example, in the section on Buddhism in '*Kirchen, Sekten Religion*' (Church, Sect, Religion),[12] there were explanations of the general history of Buddhism, of the three main schools of Buddhism (Theravada, Mahayana, and Vajirayana), and on Western Buddhism and other sects, wherein the objectives and circumstances of the religions were elaborated. Following this, a detailed classification of the three main schools and Zen, the affiliation of all groups in the German language sphere, and a simple explanation were provided. Almost all groups under Tibetan Buddhism covered the Western people as well. All public relations activities that advertise religious diversity follow in the lines of this dictionary. It actively advertises the positive aspects of religious plurality and coexistence by identifying and classifying many religions and describing the exotic aspects of these religions. In the city of Lucerne, universities conduct activities to advertise the city's religious pluralism to its citizens. In a pamphlet with colour photos, all religious groups in the city and suburbs of the Canton of Lucerne are classified into Judaism, Islam, Buddhism, Hinduism and others, each having their own logo and the location of each group printed on the map. Moreover, a photo is included in the explanations of the groups. This pamphlet is distributed all over the city and to tourist information offices in an appeal to religious pluralism. The most popular event is a bus tour that visits these religious institutions that is conducted three or four times a year. I participated in the tour in November 2005 and visited the assembly hall of Hindu Tamil immigrants, a temple that was built in a house bought by Vietnamese immigrants, and a prayer hall (cultural centre) of Muslims from Macedonia and Kosovo. All of these institutions were located in places where their existence could not be known from the outside, therefore it was a great experience in terms of getting to know of the existence of a number of different unknown religions in the city. At each location, a student who was the tour conductor read a brief explanation of the religion and the participants were allowed to look around for a short period of time. We were told about the history, doctrine and rituals of each religion,

11 *Humbert, Claude Alain* (ed.): Religionsführer Zürich, Zürich 2004.
12 *Schmid, Georg* (ed.): Kirchen, Sekten, Religionen, Zürich 2003.

so it really felt like a group tour. The local papers accompany the tour from time to time to report on it, and the voices of the participants, who express their impressions and the importance of getting to know a different culture or religion, are published in the papers.[13]

Public relations activities are very important. However, from a non-European perspective, the peculiar optimism that is seen in the 'praise' for religious pluralism is of some concern. It is said that it was in the 19th century that Europe realised the pluralist form of religion. Until the 19th century, religions were differentiated between the monotheistic religions of Christianity, Judaism and Mohammedanism, and other so-called pagan religions. However, even Judaism and Islam were not widely acknowledged to be on an equal footing with Christianity, but rather it was generally held that only Christianity rightly proclaimed the one true God and was therefore rightfully the only true religion.

According to Masuzawa, comparative linguistics studies prospered with the promotion of linguistic studies of the Asian region that followed the discovery of Buddhism, and European identity was discussed in terms of various aspects.[14] The idea of 'world religion' was also born around this time. In the beginning, this idea was used to mean religion in the singular form, which referred to Christianity. However, in the first half of the 20th century, Buddhism and Islam were incorporated and thus the term became plural later on. Furthermore, the idea of 'ethnic religion' as separate from 'world religion' disappeared. If we are to consider the promotion of a plurality of religions and the placing of religions other than Christianity in the same field as Christianity to be one aspect of the formation of modern Europe, then we may perhaps consider present-day multiculturalism or religious pluralism to be the formation of a new culture in Europe. And as the decline of Christianity's dominance accelerates, the emphasis on religious pluralism becomes stronger. The optimism of these public relations activities seem to portray a wishful image of the future. However, these European ideas have become opportunities to discover other religions. In May 2006, the 'Swiss Committee on Religion' ('*Schweizerische Rat der Religionen*') was established to promote dialogue among different religions.[15] However, Christians, Muslims and Jews were the only groups invited. There was opposition, and some questioned why Buddhists and Hindus were not invited, and why only three or five religions were represented. One of the important aspects of religious pluralism is to account for as many religions as possible,

13 Gebetshäusern auf der Spur, in: Neue Luzerner Zeitung, 23. 05. 2005; Besuch in der Moschee – Kein Wort zu heißen Themen, in: Neue Luzerner Zeitung, 20. 02. 2006, p. 27.

14 *Masuzawa, Tomoko*: The Invention of World Religion. Or, How European Universalism Was Preserved in the Language of Pluralism, Chicago 2005. With the findings from comparative linguistic studies, the following "language families" were discovered, and Europe was being formed linguistically: Indo-European, Indo-Germanic and Aryan.

15 *Rutishauser Sj, Christian M.*: Vom Religionspluralismus zum Dialog. Interreligiöse Initiativen in der Schweiz, p. 798, in: Stimmen der Zeit, No. 12, Vol. 131, 2006, pp. 795-808.

and to allow these religions to stand in the same playing field and to try to understand each other. As a result, those movements that are not considered to have religious connotations in the regions of their origin, such as Zen and yoga, are promoted to the status of 'religion'. And the spiritual culture of people who do not originally have a word for religion is fostered as 'religion'.[16]

I mentioned at the beginning of this section that "although the same term 'multireligious' is used, the present problem lies not with religion itself but with those who are in charge of it (immigrants)." This is because Western Buddhists are not normally included in multiculturalism. However, religious pluralism places a high value on plurality of culture (religion). An event called 'Religions in Lucerne, the City and the Suburbs' was hosted in Lucerne in May 2005. There was a bus tour planned for this event, and the Tibetan Buddhism Center was included in the tour. This center is not a religious institution for immigrants, but merely a simple room set amongst the city buildings where Swiss people go. This center is mainly used as a place to listen to lectures on Buddhist doctrine, but many Tibetans probably do not think that this is the same 'religion' as theirs. In an appeal to religious pluralism, Tibetan Buddhism as a religion, and not those who practice it (not necessarily immigrants), is the important point. If this is the basic idea underlying religious pluralism, it may not be so absurd for the author to link the religious pluralism of the present day with Hellenistic culture, and with India and China. However, it is clear that we cannot consider the situation to be the same among contemporary Europe, and India, China, and the Hellenistic Age, especially when taking into account issues such as what is deemed religion or who decides what religion is.

Class Stratification

What is multiculturalism or religious pluralism? It is something fundamentally different than the religious plurality seen in the early Roman Age, the Hellenistic Age, and modern day India and China. Multiculturalism is not simply a state where religions coexist in a society or region, but a phenomenon that is born from class stratification, that is, between immigrants and the host society or between the minority and the majority. This can be replaced by class stratification between the non-West and the West. That is to say, multiculturalism does not have much of a *raison d'être* if there is no class stratification. Rather, multiculturalism is camouflaged as a form of respect for other cultures in order to conceal class stratification. The public relations activities promoted in the name of religious pluralism focused on in this paper appear at first sight to reflect something other than this class-stratification-based, modern-day, Western European form of multiculturalism, but rather appear to hearken back to times when religions truly coexisted on an equal footing, such as in the early Roman Age, the Hellenistic Age, and in ancient China. It seems

16 Tibetan Buddhism was once called Lamaism, but today it has been 'promoted' to a religion and is being referred to as 'Tibetan Buddhism'.

as if immigrants and the host society are trying to welcome diversity by attempting to stand in the same playing field or even to stand side by side. However, even here, class stratification between the non-West and West exists. This may be referred to as a stratification of intellect. Christian religious concepts are applied to many cultures, which are accounted for in that manner. Daniel Valentine has referred to the influence of Christianity upon the world in the following way: "the 'conquered' in their turn have clamored to prove that they too, even as their conquerors claim, have 'religion'. With formidable help from Orientalists, Indologists, scholars of comparative religion and anthropologists, the West and the westernised have come to hold that, despite evidence to the contrary, all the peoples of the world have religion."[17] Would it be radical to think that the religious ideas of Christianity that expanded throughout the world through translations, colonisation and the proselytising of missionaries are in turn continuously being carried on by the ideology of multiculturalism in the present times? It is necessary to focus on the point that the stratification of intellect originally developed outside Europe is now being continued inside Europe at the present time. Multiculturalism does not negate class stratification, but rather class stratification is intrinsic to multiculturalism itself. Therefore, I would like to point out that multiculturalism is not necessarily at the polar opposite of assimilation.

This is not meant to be an objection to Western thought or public relations activities. Rather, the relations between the non-West and the West will always contain this element, although we are not necessarily conscious of it in everyday life. I have already mentioned that Japanese people have difficulties when asked about their religion, but we do not think that the cause of this is due to translation. In most cases, it is because our 'religious consciousness' is very low. For those people who cannot simply explain their spiritual culture with the word religion, it is somewhat strange that Buddhism has been accounted for as a religion in Europe. If one is to recognise that multiculturalism and assimilation are not polar opposites, then it is necessary to account for and at the same time place all religions on the same playing field, and to question whether religions other than Christianity can be discussed in terms of Western ideas, as well as to consider all elements relative to the context of multiculturalism instead of just supporting diversity. This also refers to the concepts of 'dialogue' and 'understanding', which are great challenges to multiculturalism. There is a research network concerning religious pluralism called 'The Pluralism Project' based at Harvard University in the U.S., and on their website one will first come across an explanation written by Diana L. Eck, titled *What is Pluralism.*[18] She states that "Pluralism is not diversity alone, but the energetic engagement with diversity [...] pluralism is not tolerance, but the active seeking for under-

17 *Valentine* 2001, p. 85.

18 *Eck, Diana L.*: What is Pluralism?, in: The Pluralism Project at Harvard University; http://www.pluralism.org/pluralism/what_is_pluralism.php [15. 10. 2010].

standing across lines of difference [...] pluralism is not relativism, but the encounter of communities [...] pluralism is based on dialogue."[19] These four points are raised as challenges to pluralism. It seems as though this train of thought regarding multiculturalism is common and not limited to the U.S. In Switzerland, the recent practices of religious pluralism not only increased awareness of religious diversity but also resulted in an increase in spaces where active dialogues are promoted to lead to understanding.[20]

In the same way that the meaning of 'religion' never was questioned and thus penetrated through other cultures as a transparent term, 'understanding' is also referred to as being self-evident. That is to say, "understanding and knowledge symbolise power, and misunderstanding, ignorance and disarrangement are useless and negative and as such to be overcome in the modern West."[21] Misunderstanding was conceived as something negative; therefore its possibilities were never pursued. A series of elements are necessary in order to understand something – for example, words, expressions, knowledge, distance between the self and other. Even though immigrants from the non-West may obtain a Western education, it is not necessarily the case that their standards are exactly the same as those of Western people. If so, then whose understanding is it that is presumed here? The stratification of knowledge reoccurs in this scenario. As it is necessary to once again consider religious concepts in terms of relativism, should we not presume misunderstanding rather than understanding?

Unraveling Culture

An event called 'The Zurich of Hindu: A Journey of Discovery' ('*Hinduistisches Zürich: Eine Entdeckungsreise*') was held in Zurich from 22 December 2004 to 28 February 2005.[22] The organisers had take many things into consideration before the event. Where should we start and end when covering 3,000 years of history? Indeed, 'Hinduism' is a concept that was created in the West in the 19th century. All books written on the subject are based on Western scholarship. It is not easy to grasp the concept. Hinduism is not only a religion, but a combination of various aspects including practices in daily lives. How should we go about examining the complex contents of this concept? The organisers of the event tried to discover some answers through the Hindu people living in Switzerland at present. Instead of referring to philosophy or rituals, they took into account the individual meaning of Hinduism. During the preparation stage, when the organisers called for the "Hindu way of life", many of the exhibitions gathered there somewhat unorthodox. How-

19 Ibid.

20 *Rutisbauser* 2006.

21 *Ochiai, Kazuyasu*: I have Nothing Special to Say. On the Invisible Violence of Cogitas Ergo Es in Intercultural Dialogue, p. 97, in: Social Identities, No. 1, Vol. 12, pp. 95-106.

22 *Belz, Johannes*: Hinduistisches Zürich. Eine Entdeckungsreise, in: Internationales Asienforum, No. 3-4, Vol. 36, Freiburg im Breisgau 2005, pp. 251-263.

ever, the organisers utilised these exhibitions and asked the participants to hold cooking classes and yoga classes. The organisers focused on the individual rather than the group or ethnic unit, in order to understand their religious identity. This was done specifically to eliminate unconscious stereotypes that are expressed in the word Hindu. In other words, the organisers felt that it was more important to discover diversity in their expression, rather than to aim for unity or dialectical integration.[23]

In order to reflect this, the organisers asked Swiss people that practiced Hinduism to participate in this event. This is because Hinduism is not an exclusively ethnic phenomenon. However, this led to unforeseen troubles, contrary to the intention of the organisers. Some sects are antagonistic to other groups such as the Hare Krishna, for example, in which Western people participate. There was also criticism against followers of Sai Baba. However, the organisers requested tried to avoid trouble and adamantly emphasised the interpretation of the individual meaning of Hinduism.

The event was not conducted on the premise of Hinduism as religion. The organisers intended to promote a condition which to some may have been interpreted as religion and to some not, and tried to express the obscure world that people live in from the individual's point of view. In non-Western cultural spheres such as Japan and China, the word religion has been translated into the native tongue, and afterwards the inhabitants of these regions have attempted to explain their culture though the use of this term. At the same time, however, the concept of religion has been applied to spiritual cultures of the non-West in Europe. It is necessary to be cautious of the idea that the West is always constant (universal) and that the non-West has been overly influenced by the West. Immigrants who live as guests in the host society of the West are even more strongly influenced by Western understanding, through the various representations that they come into contact on a daily basis and through policies such as multiculturalism. Is there no other alternative but for the guest to adapt to the host? In order to seek for ways to improve relations with immigrants, it may be necessary for the host societies to question such premises and their ideas, and for Europe to unravel some of the concepts it has created.

23 Ibid., p. 253.

References

Baumann, Martin: Viele Religionen schaden der Gesellschaft nicht. Von den Gefahren und Chancen der Religionspluralität, in: Neue Zürcher Zeitung, 29. 01. 2005

Belz, Johannes: Hinduistisches Zürich. Eine Entdeckungsreise, in: Internationales Asienforum, No. 3-4, Vol. 36, Freiburg im Breisgau 2005, pp. 251-263

Bolzman, Claudio et al.: La population âgée immigrée face à la retraite. Problème social et problématiques de recherche, in: *Hans-Rudolf Wicker* (ed.): Das Fremde in der Gesellschaft. Migration, Ethnizität und Staat/L'altérité dans la société: migration, ethnicité, État, Zürich 1996, pp. 123-142

Casanova, José: Einwanderung und der neue religiöse Pluralismus, in: Leviathan. Berliner Zeitschrift für Sozialwissenschaft, No. 2, Vol. 34, 2006, pp. 188-191

Eck, Diana L.: What is Pluralism?, in: The Pluralism Project at Harvard University; http://www.pluralism.org/pluralism/what_is_pluralism.php [15. 10. 2010]

Humbert, Claude Alain (ed.): Religionsführer Zürich, Zürich 2004

Masanori, Naito: Challenge to the West? Awakening of Muslims Immigrants in Western European Countries at the UNU-UNESCO International Conference on the Dialogue of Civilizations, Tokyo 2001

Masuzawa, Tomoko: The Invention of World Religion. Or, How European Universalism Was Preserved in the Language of Pluralism, Chicago 2005

Ochiai, Kazuyasu: I have Nothing Special to Say. On the Invisible Violence of Cogitas Ergo Es in Intercultural Dialogue, in: Social Identities, No. 1, Vol. 12, pp. 95-106

Rutishauser Sj, Christian M.: Vom Religionspluralismus zum Dialog. Interreligiöse Initiativen in der Schweiz, in: Stimmen der Zeit, No. 12, Vol. 131, 2006, pp. 795-808

Schmid, Georg (ed.): Kirchen, Sekten, Religionen, Zürich 2003

Valentine, Daniel E.: The Arrogation of Being by The Blind-Spot of Religion, in: Hitotsubashi Journal of Social Studies, No. 1, Vol. 33, 2001, pp. 83-102

Recasting the Vision of Megacities in the South. Emerging Challenges for the North-South Dialogue in Development

Sheela Patel

The city is the location where many sets of forces that seek to shape it clash. This battle operates on many levels. The city's history battles with its present and future forms. Its different inhabitants battle for space and dominance, local trade battles with global trade and international forces battle with local forces. They battle with each other and with forces from outside to produce a unique character or 'persona' of the city. This makes the city a dynamic and ever-changing space, with different actors vying with each other, all seeking to play their own roles in the shaping of the city.

Many cities today have character, a specific imagery that is projected onto it. Yet despite this seemingly static description, at every moment there are massive forces seeking to change the nature, character and substance of the city. Depending on what your paradigm or perspective is, you may approve or disapprove of the forces that seek to bring change. Megacities such as Mumbai, Mexico City, Tokyo, Sao Paulo and New York are cities with a population of over 10 million. In the next year or so, more than half of the world will be living in urban areas. Many new megacities will emerge, almost all of them in the south. And many rural areas will become urban via changes in the occupation of the residents. Many small towns will become part of metropolitan regions by being sucked into the vortex of demands and expectations of these large cities. Most growth, they say, will be in medium- and small-sized towns, but these large megacities will dominate the economic climate of their nations. They will become the gateway of their nations' discourse with global forces, and sometimes they will change the discourse, but they will always be transformed by the external economical impact of investments that pass through them.

Germany, I am told, does not have any megacities. It has very few high-rise buildings, but is clearly fascinated by them. German architects and engineers routinely get contracts to build megamalls and skyscrapers in other countries, and soon German and European businesses and investors will begin to invest in these large cities in the south, seeking new markets and new investment opportunities as the world economy opens up and make these new locations accessible. What is clear is that the global trade policy framework designed to circulate money and markets is well ahead of the policy framework designed to address issues of equity, protection of human rights and to ensure protection of social, cultural and indigenous institutions, practices and processes. Political leadership in the north and south is obsessed with economic growth and the health of markets, but has little capacity or imagination to regulate markets so that they are also responsible for these issues. As a result, cities all over the world are facing the death of their culture and character. They are literally becoming homogenised like those cities in computer games, where houses, malls, fast food and international fashion make wherever you are seem the same. It is a culture where sameness is security and diversity is frightening.

Many people excited by the growth and the wealth produced now claim that the world is flat. They falsely assume that opportunities and resources are now globally available to all. This neglects the reality that this wealth and the opportunity to produce it are unequally distributed, and the difference between the rich and the poor within a locality, within nations and among nations has grown faster than ever before. This has huge implications on various fronts. The enormous gap between rich and poor, the ever-deepening divide between the demands for better infrastructure for the rich and the access to basic amenities for the poor stands out most.

Globalisation is producing greater informality and lesser provisions for health and income security. Globalisation, however, is producing huge consumption demands among all youth in the north and south, yet with divergent possibilities of accessing resources. The ones with access to incomes have the purchasing power, and purchase and consume. The lack of income leads to increasing violence and break-ins. People steal and sometimes kill for consumer goods. While creating wealth, cities have become unsafe. Violence and crime in cities is somehow not linked to the real issues of breaking down communities, fragmentation of identity and the seduction of consumerism.

Cities are also becoming unsustainable. They suck more water from their vicinity, often leaving those living closest to the water with shortages and drought. They waste water while transporting it, and the final consumer in turn has no knowledge of or responsibility for conservation. While most of these cities would be proud to show that they have adequate per capita water, in reality one third of the population will be using four fifths of the water. Cities produce more waste, further degrading and polluting their environment and water bodies, and crucial areas such as mangroves and forests are cut down to expand the footprint of the city.

Global capital is the new hallowed visitor that cities seek to seduce. Cities all around the world are rated for quality of life, for access to good infrastructure, for their global finances and for their companies and staff. City managers compete to make investments to attract capital. This is often at the cost of local equity, because these gains come at the cost of depriving someone else.

All cities need and tacitly encourage migrants to come and do the work the residents of the city don't want to do cheaply. Migration, the UN tells us in a recent report, is something to pay heed to. Populations have always moved to seek better opportunities and improved living conditions. Whether migrants are internal (from within the country) or transnational, they produce a wide spectrum of changes. In almost all instances the labour of migrants is welcomed, but the resident population would like the migrants to be invisible the rest of the time. Invariably, they impact the social, political and cultural life of the cities they migrate to, and in all occasions this threatens the local population and makes them feel insecure. The capacity to manage such diversity requires political and cultural leadership, most of which seems to have vanished in an era of seeking political gain through the polarisation of populations.

Be it Davos or Nairobi, both the World Economic Forum and the World Social Forum are sending out messages that economic growth is hollow when not accompanied by social and cultural transformations. Nations at war, regions facing civil wars, and cities where local populations are in a state of unrest need political solutions that money and investments alone cannot buy. Peace and safety are needed, and we are all in pursuit of cities that have the capacity to absorb differences among cultures and that can thus celebrate diversity. How will this come about? In a consumerist environment seeking more and more individualised identities and gain, how can the society of the 21st century be envisaged? Will the media, together with its consumerism and the self-centeredness it promotes, allow society to explore alternatives to rejuvenate itself?

For many decades development pundits across the world have maligned cities and sought to reverse urbanisation. Yet cities are powerful and dynamic spaces that cannot be wished away – at least not in this century. Their power will wax and wane, but they are a critical part of nations, and most nations that have healthy GDPs are more than 60 % urban. So it is important to understand the emerging cities of the south, and the forces that forge their character are worth exploring. Many divergent forces provide the energy and the character of the city. Its governance and its commitment to equity, its ability to manage and reconcile differences have to be located within the city. The way it encourages its residents to contribute to peace and harmony while undertaking a wide spectrum of activities is vital for the cities of tomorrow. In the coming year, the world will turn urban. More people will live in cities than ever before.

Most of the urbanisation is expected to take place in Africa, and it will also be high in South Asia and China. In Africa, migration is beginning to occur to cities that are already facing huge deficits. In South Asia, especially India and China, countries are in high growth brackets, yet inequity is still a major issue. Most of the migrants coming to cities will be poor, with very few skills and no funds or assets except their labour. Most of the cities already have a negative relationship with their poor, and have already deployed their resources inequitably. The cities are two cities, the formal and the informal. The inhabitants share the same geography, and ever so often the formal city will invade the informal areas, as it demands more space and resources, believing that it does not hold responsibility for the consequences of its actions. In the past, this has produced huge waves of evictions in neighbourhoods, and this trend can be expected to increase in the future.

Each section of the city can give its version of how it seeks to bring changes to itself and its environment, and to change the city to ensure spaces for itself. They can narrate their engagement so that the external or global forces in turn engage with the city. So today I will share with you the version of transformation that the urban poor seek to bring about in order to have the city work for them.

Let's take the city of Bombay, or Mumbai, as our politicians would like to call it. I have lived in that city all my life and speak all three languages that are spoken there. If you speak in Marathi, the language of the province or state of Maharashtra, you say 'Mumbai'. If you speak Hindi, which is our national language, you say 'Bumbai', which was the name the Portuguese gave it. And when you speak in English, you say 'Bombay'. Many of us see this as a sign of the cosmopolitan character of the city, which we are proud of. One section of the city, the Marathi-speaking sons of the soil and their political party, the Shiv Sena, seek to have this city serve the interests of the Maharashtrians. So when they came to power in 1995, they changed the name of the city. Now all of the metropolitan cities of India are changing their names to 'Indian' names while going global! So 'Bangalore' became 'Bengaluroo', 'Calcutta' became 'Kolkotta', 'Madras' became 'Chennai', and so on. We all wait with bated breath for Delhi to change its name as well. Paradoxically, the same groups of people are also seeking FDI and increased investment of global players in the city. For those who don't know the history of Bombay: It was a series of seven fishing islands off the western coast of the western part of the peninsula. Around 1600, these marshy fishing villages and the areas surrounding them were leased to the Portuguese by the King of Kutch. Around 1800, it was passed on to the British Empire as part of the dowry of a Portuguese princess who married the English King. Its natural harbor was of use to the British who needed a port for transporting goods from India and to India from Britain, and also for trade with China. A city sprung up to support the port. Shipbuilders and traders were brought from Gujarat, which is north of the city, and workers were brought from the hinterland of what is now the state of Maharashtra to work in the shipbuilding yards and later in the textile mills. This explains why the working class is from Maharashtra and the business elite from Gujarat. These two states were originally called Bombay State and were split into two in the 1960s, with the City going to Bombay, despite many efforts by the Gujarati businessmen to make it part of Gujarat.

The design of the city was simple. The British carved out spaces for themselves, their port, the industries to feed the port, their business areas and the residential area. Adjoining the latter was the Indian quarter, where all the mills were, and around them were tenements built for the workers to stay in because, ironically, at that time they had to be persuaded to come and work in the city. The city had its municipal corporation provide (as in Victorian London) a council to assist its traders in the late 1800s. Along with Karachi, it was the second municipal corporation in India. The first sewer system was not established to be of service to the population, but because the Egyptian consulate had informed the municipal commissioner in 1890 that the plague was being transported through rats to Egypt via the ships used to trade cotton, and that their ships would no longer dock in Bombay!

The seven islands were joined, two railway lines were set up for the transportation of goods to the hinterland, and the southernmost tip was where the formal city with its Victorian stone buildings represented the trademark of Britannia. After the Native quarter came the informal city, in which those who serviced the city and its elite resided. There was some invisible line, almost apartheid-like, beyond which they lived, and as the city needed more land these residents were pushed back to make space for the formal city.

Every community and every district of India is represented in Bombay. And every decade saw many more who came from all over the country in search of livelihood and a better life for their children. Every household remembers its origins and dons many identities, that of language, caste, religion, region – even the slum dwellers. They tell their histories of migration, of forced evictions and amazing survival despite the city's destruction of their land. Why did they stay in the city? Because they had no choice. There were no jobs in the villages, no life, no food. Collecting waste in the city got them a better income than working all day as farm labour. Many could remove their sense of untouchability as they used public transportation and wore city clothes. However, even today most of the slum dwellers belong to backward castes.

The overall trajectory of the city's development is also the story of evictions and the accidental formations of small and large clusters of slum dwellers in various parts of the city, which can claim today to have half of its total population of 12 million living in slums. When people were evicted, they had no rights, no protection, so they moved from that location to another one, either formally or informally as directed by the administration. Dharavi, which was way outside the city in the early 1920s, was formed when groups of Tamilians who cured leather settled there to procure the skins of animals slaughtered in a nearby abattoir to make leather. A similar number of families came from Uttar Pradesh to work on railway construction. They cleared the marshes and built their houses. Over the next fifty years, some communities like the potters came and settled there. Others who were evicted from other locations were given a nod that they could live there. The fisher folk, which are some of the original residents of the city, found their village engulfed in slums. Dharavi was outside Bombay until 1956, but by 1974 it had fully become part of the city as the latter engulfed it and advanced to outer areas. Even though the city surrounded it, it had no amenities or services or roads going through it, only pathways beaten through the bush by the needs of the residents to reach the outside of Dharavi. It was in the 1970s that, less for serving the poor than for providing easier access to the newly formed suburbs, the first roads were carved out of Dharavi. Its growth was now restricted by the two railway stations on two sides and the roads that triangulated it. The identity of the residents could be classified in many ways – by the origin of their migration, their caste, their occupation, their religion and their language. They also had identities by neighbourhoods or Nagars or cooperatives, but to the rest of the city they were simply residents of Dharavi.

Dharavi is the archetypal slum that emerges as soon as anyone brings forth the issue of slums. It is often portrayed as the largest slum in Asia. To the present day, the exact numbers of its residents, structures, families and businesses have not accurately been calculated, nor have its numbers been accepted by the city and its residents. In 1974, Charles Corea, a well-respected and world-famous Indian architect, was given the task of upgrading Dharavi. He suggested investments to provide Dharavi with basic amenities and also suggested supporting its upgrading with community participation. But nothing much happened. Then, as the Congress Party of India was celebrating its centenary in Bombay, the then prime minister of India, Rajeev Gandhi, gave Rs. 100 crores (Rs. 1,000 million), of which 35 crores was for the transformation of Dharavi. Many plans were made, and in the end some buildings were built, many without storm water drains and that therefore let water in. But Dharavi survived that phase and retained its nature and character.

Today, in 2007, the government has yet another plan, one which is more difficult and dangerous for the residents. The government plan has divided Dharavi into sectors, and leaves aside the buildings already constructed. 44 of the existing 240 hectares would be redeveloped, so that the present residents would get 21 square meters of tenements free of charge, while the rest of the space would be developed to provide additional housing. That would subsidise the housing for the residents, and also provide money to government and the developers, as all development would be taken up by international bidders.

Initially, the residents chose to ignore these plans. Residents said that many had come and tried to change Dharavi, and that this was simply another one of those plans. But unlike in the past, when the plans belonged to the government and its inefficient housing authority, the present situation was different. Each Sector will be open to bidding from global development companies who will first compete with each other over how much money to give the government to develop this place. Then they have to plan and design their sector. When the state and the private sector get together, where does it leave the residents? Many questions come up for discussion and reflections. Shouldn't those who have created Dharavi, its residents, be involved in re-visioning it? Is the government's present form of consultations, i. e. showing residents PowerPoint presentations, akin to their acceptance of the plan?

The next question is: Is this kind of development good for the city? Most poor people will categorically say that they are uncomfortable about how many questions this process does not answer. The government and the consultants say they have made many presentations to the residents to tell them about the plan. The residents argue that telling them what the government planned is not the same as creating a dialogue and discussion within which they could state their opinions and participate in the process. This is their prerogative, having developed Dharavi from scratch, even if they are too poor to participate in all aspects of the process. Clearly, the number crunchers see huge deals and profit. Does the government really believe that the residents will be satisfied with just a 21 square meter tenement?

The residents have many other concerns. First of all they know that the basic bulk services are not able to meet even a mere 30 % of their needs. How will the plan provide for the additional requirements? The government argues that the city is planning to get more water (seven years later), and that the developers who win the bids have to provide all bulk services. Yet the poor do not believe that this will be done. While the state itself has a terrible record of qualitative and quantitative delivery, the private sector is even less accountable. How can they believe this will change now?

The residents are upset about the manner in which the present plan has assumed very few non-residential or production units, and does not take into account the huge diversity of businesses that are presently able to employ people both within Dharavi and outside of it. With state institutions taking no responsibility in dealing with employment, most poor people live in fragile occupational situations that cannot be reconstituted once they are destroyed. The formal city administration is not taking this into account. How, it asks, could the state take responsibility for that?

The upper-class residents of Bombay see nothing wrong in this. The slum dwellers will get a decent house, they say. And since the location of Dharavi is next to the new business district, it can attract investment and produce additional real estate. The residents are upset. Who developed Dharavi, they asked? How are we different from the others to whom the city has given land in the past for development? Why, if this kind of development has to be done, are our rights to develop and share in the profits not accepted?

The city of Bombay is the state of Maharashtra's golden goose. Because most businesses and banks have their headquarters in the city, it is always looking for a makeover. First it aspired to be Singapore, and now Shanghai! The state government has failed to transform the city's slums in the past, and has been hard pressed for dealing with slum upgrading. However, with no history of good data, lack of capacity to dialogue with the poor, and the inability to demonstrate transparency to produce community trust in state planning, a huge challenge remains before it. As I write this paper, municipal elections are about to be held (in a week's time), and the residents who had elected all congress counselors in Dharavi are angry with their politicians because they have not supported the community's right to participate in that transformation. And soon after the election, the global tenders will be out and the bids will come in.

Every few years there is a battle like this. Sustainable development activists and pro-poor movements generally fail to get the state to agree to a solution that produces a win-win situation in the city. And this time, too, there is an attempt to work with local communities to produce a strategy for participation in which the residents have a say and can contribute to the process of change. How can this reconciliation occur?

To some, this example demonstrates the blip in the development of the city. To others, it is one more way to obliterate the cosmopolitan nature and character of the city that resides in its poor neighbourhoods, for many of us see a pattern in what is happening. Last year a huge battle was lost when all those who fought for the use of land on which textile mills (which were all closed) stood to be used as open spaces, and to provide public housing. Now all those mills are going to produce high-rise gated communities and change what was a working class neighbourhood into a gentrified one. Parallel to the battle for Dharavi is the land which belonged to the Bombay Port, which is now being sold bit by bit again for private use, denying the city access to the eastern water front.

Almost all of the city's recycling and waste separation has been done in Dharavi; almost every industry in the city has some linkages with Dharavi. It is a township within a city, and a microcosm of the heart of the city. It does not want to wait to be homogenised and steadily gentrified, thereby allowing the formal city to engulf another of its historic milestones. It is one more demonstration of how the city does not work for the benefit of all its residents, and of how politicians forget their responsibility to arbitrate between the different demands of the city.

The capacity to retain the cosmopolitan character of the city is at stake, and the diverse culture that makes up the city stands vulnerable in the face of global financial capital. How will the spaces be kept so as to nurture diversity for all, making them culturally vibrant? What are the challenges of understanding issues of ethnic diversity and multiple aspirational compulsions that produce the dense and complex energy that we call 'city' today?

We all know that the real challenge of this century is poverty and inequity. Cities cannot be shielded or protected from the poor who come to seek aspirational transformations of their lives. The development of cities is like looking at a glass – is it half-full or half-empty? Can the political, intellectual and social leadership see an opportunity to address poverty by making cities capable of dealing with the poor who come into them? Can they create a ladder for their inclusion into the city? What can the provide for its poorer residents while benefiting from their skills and labour? Can the capacity to strengthen due processes that ensure good governance become the norm rather than the exception? Can northern cities and countries deal with their poor, whose ranks have been growing disproportionately in recent decades, in similar ways? And can those of us who care bring about the reconciliation between economic and other developments to produce a well-rounded and evolving society that cares for all?

These reflections have a huge impact on the demands we make on our local and global leaders, opinion makers and social movements. These crucial choices of inclusion or exclusion, of coexistence or violence have major implications. At the turn of the last century, countries joined together to make the millennium declaration to halve poverty, but little has emerged from that political promise.

I am part of a support group for national federations of the urban poor who have decided to take charge of their destinies and unite as slum dwellers that have been excluded in cities. They seek to engage the state to produce inclusive strategies for the poor in cities. It is a long and difficult task, because the poor have to develop both skills and confidence in order to be able to demand a dialogue with the city and the state. They have to sustain their capacity for mobilisation and cohesion when they face short-term failures, which will always crop up as cities do not easily engage or develop strategies for the poor. This transformation is a response to globalisation, because while there is a demonstrable attempt to decentralise administration and political control, the strategies, resources and development discourse are still controlled by distant transnational institutions, most of which are inaccessible to the poor. By creating organisations that have sub-district levels, city levels and national levels in their leadership structures, and which have now aggregated into a transnational organisation, which they call Shack Dwellers International, the SDI seeks to bring the voice of the poor into a range of discourses that ultimately shape their cities and their future status in their communities.

Set up in 1996, the SDI is now ten years old. It was set up by eight national federations that learnt from each other and shared views and strategies and supported each other in their national and international negotiations. This organisation has internal capacity building functions. It has begun dialogues with regional and continental associations of ministers, mayors, and financial organisations financing development in their cities, and has now begun to participate in a global discourse about urban poverty.

They are successful, at times, but what they have begun to do is change the nature of the discourse at committee meetings and events because their presence at these various levels demands that the accountability, which had been only lip service to the poor before, is now validated with demonstrable outcomes in which these or similar institutions are involved. But more importantly, the SDI champions the transformation that is possible in cities that are inclusive. Development discourse, even today, is mainly rural. There is a deep-seated belief that the urban is bad, that urbanisation needs to be reversed, and that successful development means people going back to villages. Well, data and statistics show that this is not going to happen, and in reality urban and rural lives and linkages have to be seen in a continuum giving everyone a chance to retain all linkages and provide support to retain kinship associations across urban and rural spaces, whether in the north, south, east or west. This was made clear when New York City stated it was proud to be the second home to the largest number of people – thus celebrating diversity.

In conclusion, let us consider what this talk brings to the deliberations of this conference. First of all, it would seem to me that there is an urgent need to go beyond a simple "we are German and we wish to have a dialogue with you and others." The Germans here, as with all other participants, all carry many cultures and identities, and we need to explore and celebrate those.

Culture is a word that is often treated with disrespect in the harsh and competitive world of markets and finances. The world of markets does not acknowledge that it too presents a domineering culture which, if it does not respect and celebrate other manifestations of culture, will itself lose ground. Violence of the disenfranchised can destroy economic gains, and cities, as we know, can go up in flames with the rage of that discontent. Culture and heritage are not just buildings and things of the past. They are the vibrant, present and dynamic relationships, rituals and practices that produce institutions, capacities, mechanisms and the ability to arbitrate and engage. We have to challenge ourselves to explore this without fear or mistrust.

When Illusion Meets Reality: The Evolving Relationship Between China and Europe

Minxin Pei

Like my distinguished predecessor who spoke one moment ago here, I was also a transplanted American. I adopted America and America adopted me. So my view is colored by both sides, as I grew up in China and live in America. I spent the last 22 years in the US, first as a graduate student and now as academic. I hope to give you a spontaneous speech without notes because I believe that to be more analytical. Nevertheless, I want to start with some notes.

With regards to the title of the conference and my European experiences, I want to say that I have been to Europe many times. The Europeans, like the peoples of most other continents, want to know what outsiders think of them, which is quite understandable. Although many people tend to be skeptical about Europe, about its potential and its accomplishments, I believe that Europe has accomplished a great deal. And this is something that the Chinese tend to think about when it comes to Europe.

China is nominally a communist country, but when the Chinese come to Europe, they realise that Europe has achieved socialism with a human face. It is Europe that has sound environment policies, universal access to health care and education; in Europe you have job security – of course at a very high price – but you also have the highest level of equality among developed countries. And you have, compared to other democratic countries, the least corrupt governments. These are all very important accomplishments. That's where I would say that Europe has special advantages and will continue to have them because Europe has that unique brand of soft power that the US and other countries do not have. First, you have the power of example: you lead by higher standards. Second, you have the power of leadership. Even though Europe does not have the same amount of power as the US, Europe does lead in some of the most critical areas of global governance, especially on the issue of global warming. You also have the power of generosity. Europe is the most generous donor with regards to development assistance in the world, after adjustments for GDP (gross domestic product) more generous than the United States. And Europe also offers the power of hope. The US, where I have spent the last 22 years, offers the hope of individual achievement. But Europe offers the hope of collective welfare as well. With Europe, we can see the possibility that national identities can indeed be overcome. You *can* form something that lies beyond the narrowness of nationalism. This is why I think Europe truly is not only cross-national, it is postmodern. I would say that it offers a higher level of hope. This, then, is what an outsider thinks of Europe.

Now let me come to a more practical issue, namely Europe's relationship with China. I would say that Europe's most important relationship today is with the US. There is no doubt about that. But with which country does Europe have its second most important relationship? Here, I think the contenders are Russia and China. If you take away the energy equation with regards to Russia, then you would have to say that China is Europe's most important country, next to the US. This is because the economic relationship between Europe and China is much more intensive and growing. Today, China is Europe's largest trading partner; it conducts more trade with China than with the US. At the end of last year, it was about 270 billion dollars with a growth rate of about 10 % a year. In its dealings with China, Europe has also had lots of difficulties. Europe does not have a good grasp of the China it is dealing with. China does not have a good understanding of the kind of Europe it is dealing with. I would say that this is because China and Europe operate on very different philosophies of foreign policy and geopolitics. Europe is quintessentially liberal. China is quintessentially realist. This is a very ironic situation. China and the US are in an extremely competitive relationship. The US sees China as its biggest potential rival, a threat. China sees the US as a threat to its continued development. But strangely, China and the US know how to handle each other, because they share the same philosophy in their dealing with one another. Both of them understand, appreciate and respect hard power. They do not have much room for soft power. Yet Europe, in dealing with China, has had a great deal of difficulties, for Europe operates on the basis of soft power, on the basis of international liberalism, while China operates on the opposite end of the spectrum; it operates in the realm of realism. That is why I think that the two, who are both continental powers, have had an unstable start to their relationship over the last five years.

We will see that China became a truly global partner with its accession to the WTO in 2001. Before that, China was rising, but I think that joining the WTO really marked China's arrival as a global economic power. And the EU-China relationship began to develop more fully after that. But the two partners approached their relationship with unrealistic expectations or illusions at the beginning. For China, Europe is a potential pole in a multipolar world. China always wanted and still wants that, because a multipolar world will give China more power in building coalitions with other powers to counterbalance the US. China also understands that Europe does not see China as military threat. Polls in Europe consistently show that less then 30 % of Europeans see China as a military threat while in the US almost 50 to 60 % of the Americans see China as a military threat. If this is true, China's rise poses much less of a threat to Europe. That gives China more confidence in dealing with Europe. But China does not understand Europe.

First of all, as I said, China does not understand the centrality of human rights in European politics and the European conception of legitimate government. Europe measures its relationships with other parts of the world mainly through the conduct of human rights in those countries.

Second, China also poorly understands the enduring relationship across the Atlantic. It thinks that somehow this relationship can be changed by the emergence of China. China also does not understand that Europe may be socialism with a human face. Europe has not really successfully dealt with global economic challenge. Europe is much less well-equipped than the US in dealing with the rise of China as an economic power. One interesting thing emerges when you look at the polls: the Europeans do not see China as a military threat; but most Europeans do see China as an economic threat. In the US most Americans see China as a military threat but only a small percentage of Americans sees China as an economic threat. It is a chiasma of sorts.

As a result, China was not prepared for the rise of economic protectionism (with regards to Chinese imports in Europe). Obviously, illusions also existed among Europeans when they dealt with China. First, they say that an emergent China is a potential global partner for Europe in dealing with the issue of global governance. Second, they think that engaging China can transform China politically, to make the country more like Europe. It's very strange. Whenever you engage China – whether you are European or American – you want to make China more like you. The idea of converting 1.3 billion people to your belief system does indeed carry a lot of weight. Furthermore, China is a huge market. Finally, some Europeans, though not all Europeans, do believe that an emergent China can be a partner in balancing American dominance, an idea that is particularly prevalent in France and Germany. With these unrealistic expectations of each other, one can see a series of missteps between Europe and China. First of all, they claim to be in a strategic partnership with each other, without understanding what the meaning of 'strategic' and of 'partnership' really is. The Europeans decide to put aside the issue of human rights and fair trade, and they decide to honour Chinese leaders with lavish treatment, despite their poor human rights record.

And I think the particular event was the arms embargo issue. In 2004 and 2005, Europe somehow decided to lift the arms embargo against China because Europe thought China was not being treated equally, and because the arms embargo was a stigma for China. Europe imposes arms embargos on only four or five countries, and most of them are rogue states, with the exception of China.

The move to lift the embargo, which turned out to be disastrous for the Europe-China relationship, actually led to the emergence of a more healthy European understanding of China. The history of the arms embargo is quite well known, of course. The Americans were very much opposed. Some European countries were not really comfortable about lifting the embargo; so there was a debate within Europe as well.

And then the Chinese themselves did not behave exactly in a correct way. They did not give up any ground on human rights. If they had decided to, say, ratify one of the human rights treaties, that would have made a huge difference. But China tried to get something for nothing. So things did not work out. As a result, the arms embargo failure was quickly followed by rising trade tensions between Europe and China, due to the fact that trade deficits with China were rising very quickly, and also because of a textile dispute between China and Europe. So that led both China and Europe to reassess their mutual relationship. And the assessment, as I said, has produced a much better relationship between Europe and China today – better because it's more grounded in reality.

Europe now understands what China is and China understands where Europe stands. They understand, for example, that the differences between Europe and China about human rights are fundamental. As long as China is governed by a one-party system, differences between China and Europe will persist. A one-party system does treat its citizens very differently, in comparison to the way European citizens – who have a huge influence on their government policy – are treated. This makes European citizens uncomfortable dealing with a country such as China.

Second, Europe also understands that integrating China into the international system is much harder. Even in the economic field, we know that this integration is very difficult. Europe also understands that China's future is uncertain despite thirty years of rapid economic growth. China faces enormous domestic challenges in terms of environmental degradation, rising inequality, corruption of its government and rising social instability. The episode of the arms embargo also taught China that Europe and US will continue to have an enduring relationship. China also understands that for Europe the economic impact of China's rise will continue to be politically sensitive. So there's a limit to Europe's strategic partnership with China. The relationship between China and Europe is not as close as it used to be. Remember the days the Eiffel tower was lit up in Chinese red? They are gone. But the relationship today is healthier; it is based on realism and on a much better understanding between Europe and China.

So when we look at the future, we see four new problems.

First of all, there is the issue of global warming, for Europe has taken the leading role for humanity in combating global warming. The US is at the moment the big bad boy in the world in terms of greenhouse gas emissions. But we know that China is catching up quickly with the US. In 2009 China will surpass the US as the largest emitter of greenhouse gases. Sooner or later, Europe will have to confront China on global warming and on the role that China will have to play in this area. China will have to make sacrifices. We all know that, because as you might have heard – and I was there when Tony Blair said this in Davos – if the UK shuts down and does not emit another ounce of greenhouse gases, the net increase of greenhouse gases in China in two years will be more than the entire emission for the UK. This means China will have to be a player. I see this being probably one of the top three issues between Europe and China in the coming decade.

Second, there are the enormous economic imbalances caused by China's rise. The bilateral trade imbalance between Europe and China is critically unsustainable; Europe's trade deficit with China is almost 200 billion dollar. It is rising much faster than the US trade deficit with China. That will cause enormous disruption within Europe. For the US, the outsourcing of manufacturing jobs is almost complete, but that is not true for Europe, parts of which will be hit very hard, especially Italy and Spain. The other problem in the economic field is China's currency policy. Because the Chinese currency is fixed with the US dollar, the entire adjustment burden has fallen on the Euro. The Euro has risen much faster, whereas China's currency has not risen at all *vis-à-vis* the Euro. This will be another big part of the economic problem.

The third major issue is human rights, which will remain an issue between Europe and China because the Chinese leadership will not liberalise its political system. They have learned from the collapse of the Soviet Union. This collapse was the greatest positive development for Europe since the end of World War II, but the Chinese leadership understands that if they liberalise, the communist party will not be able to survive. That's the lesson. If Europe thinks that it can somehow persuade the Chinese Communist Party to be more like Gorbachev, then Europe will be bitterly disappointed. And there will be tension, because the European people will lose patience.

And finally, there is China's global role. China is a rising global power. And China today is much more active in two areas of fundamental and critical importance to Europe: first in Africa, where European developmental assistance is very important. Yet China has now become the biggest donor to Africa. How will China behave in Africa? There is also the question of energy. Europe again is a major stakeholder in global energy securities, and China's current behaviour is not exactly good news for Europe. These four issues will be a huge test for Europe. So what should Europe do?

I have three propositions. The first piece of advice I would give to Europe is to work more closely with the US. The US is Europe's true partner. With George Bush in power today, things are more difficult, but we already have seen half of a regime change in Washington; half of the government is now controlled by the Democrats. In 2008, we will have a complete regime change that will bring Europe and the US much closer together. They will become true partners.

Second, within the EU you must maintain unity on China. I would say that Chancellor Angela Merkel has a much better grasp of what kind of political system China has because the chancellor herself grew up under communism and appreciates the limits of change within a communist system. So I think that within the EU the larger countries have to reach a consensus on how to deal with China.

Third, Europe has to change the role of its engagement in China. It has been mainly uncritical engagement so far. Whenever they have wanted to criticise China, European countries have always been too timid to do so. I think in China politeness is necessary, but you have to know that uncritical engagement does not get your respect in China. You have to engage, but also be critical. Don't be afraid to criticise things that you do not believe are in accord with European values or your European interests.

Sri Lanka's Search for Sustainable Peace

Mario Gomez

Sri Lanka's ethnic war came to an abrupt end, when one of the warring parties suddenly suffered a heavy military defeat in May 2009. The end was brutal with the UN and other organisations estimating that thousands of civilians lost their lives in the final battles. For almost 30 years before that Sri Lanka had been battling the awful consequences of civil war. The war had cost lives, damaged infrastructure, destroyed families and communities, and had torn at human and inter-ethnic relationships.

The end of the violence provides a unique opportunity for the country's political leadership to address the issues of inequality, social injustice, and institutional decay that have characterised life in Sri Lanka for many years. It provides a perfect opportunity to build a plural and multi-ethnic society that fosters diversity and treasures difference.

The end of the violence also provides an opportunity for the country to deal with the atrocities of the past and to explore mechanisms for accountability, truth telling, reconciliation and healing. While the conflict snuffed out lives, maimed and displaced people, and destroyed infrastructure, it also destroyed inter-ethnic relationships, stifled childhoods and left psychological scars that will take many years to heal.

Yet the events since the end of the war in May 2009 do not raise any hope that processes of reconciliation and institutional reform will be initiated. Instead the country went through an acrimonious presidential election in January 2010 and is preparing for a parliamentary election in April 2010. Accompanying this is an unprecedented crackdown on dissent, sometimes resulting in a loss of life of the dissenter. These events suggest that the ruling regime is rather interested in consolidating its political power than in initiating any serious process of constitutional reform or ethnic healing.

Introduction

For almost 30 years Sri Lanka has been battling the horrific consequences of a civil war. The war has cost lives, damaged infrastructure, destroyed families and communities, and torn at human and inter-ethnic relationships. A ceasefire signed by the LTTE and the Government of Sri Lanka in February 2002 brought some stability and allowed over 350,000 people to return to their homes. It also facilitated a rebuilding of infrastructure and housing and eased movement between the northern and southern parts of the country. After many years the previously polarised populations of the South and North were able to travel and interact with each other. Demining initiatives began in earnest, which facilitated return for the displaced. The conflict erupted once again at the end of 2005 and then ended with the defeat of the LTTE in May 2009. The intensity of violence during the final phase of the war was worse than before, and civilian life, property and relationships were the biggest casualty.[1]

In 2006 the President Mahinda Rajapaksa established an All Party Conference (APC) to design a constitutional settlement to the country's ethnic conflict. The APC subsequently established an All Party Representative Committee (APRC) consisting of one representative from each political party and a panel of 17 constitutional experts to advise the APC on the shape and design that such a constitutional settlement should take.

The APC and APRC were established ostensibly to build a consensus among political parties in the south of the country and to agree on a framework for a political settlement that could be presented to the LTTE. It brought together all the political parties represented in the National Parliament barring the Tamil National Alliance (TNA), which has functioned as a proxy voice for the LTTE. Initially there was some hope that this process would generate an imaginative constitutional settlement. While some among the panel of experts came up with the elements of a reasonable constitutional settlement, the process collapsed.[2]

Background to the Conflict

Sri Lanka consists of seven major population groups: Sinhalese – mainly Buddhist, but also Christian; Tamils – mainly Hindu, but also Christian; Muslims; Tamils of recent Indian origin – who were brought from India to work the tea plantations and who live mainly in the central part of the country; Burghers – descendants of the Dutch, Portuguese and British who intermarried; Malays – Muslims who were part of a migration from South East Asia; and other smaller groups of minorities.

Charges of discrimination have been hurled from different groups. The Sinhalese contended that the Tamils wielded a disproportionate amount of public power when Sri Lanka was known as Ceylon and a British colony. They argued that this was part of a deliberate policy on the part of the British to 'divide and rule'. A consequence of this policy was a disproportionate number of public service appointments that was held by the Tamils, at the time of independence. It is also alleged

1 See also the *International Crisis Group*: Sri Lanka's Human Rights Crisis. Asia Report No. 135, 14. 06. 2007; http://www.crisisgroup.org/en/regions/asia/south-asia/sri-lanka/135-sri-lankas-human-rights-crisis.aspx [15. 10. 2010].

2 See *Rohan Edrisinha* et al.: Power Sharing in Sri Lanka: Constitutional and Political Documents 1926-2008 (Berghof Foundation for Conflict Studies and the Centre for Policy Alternatives), Colombo 2008, for an analysis of the APRC's proposals.

that, at the time of independence, educational and other facilities in the Northern Province, which is almost 90 % Tamil, were at a better stage of development than other predominantly Sinhalese areas. From the Tamils came allegations that there has been a consistent policy of discrimination by Sinhalese dominated governments since independence. Few government resources have been channelled into areas where Tamils reside, and they have been discriminated against with regard to the use of the Tamil language, educational opportunities, and access to public service jobs.

Violence by Sinhala Groups

Sri Lanka has experienced a number of bouts of political violence over the past 40 years. In 1971 the Janatha Vimukthi Peramuna (People's Liberation Front) or JVP sought to capture state power through a violent struggle that was crushed ruthlessly by the government at that time. In 1987 the JVP staged a comeback. During a two year period they brought the country to a halt through a series of tactics that entailed intimidation and fear. The violence came to an end in November 1989 when most of the leadership was killed. Some escaped, returned to Sri Lanka and formed a mainstream political party which is now represented in Parliament.

Violence by Tamil Groups

In 1976 a Tamil political party adopted the 'Vaddukoddai Resolution' which called for the creation of 'a free, sovereign, secular, socialist state of Tamil Eelam' based on the right of self determination inherent to every nation. The resolution argued that the Tamils had tried to live together with Sinhalese but this was not possible any more. The Vaddukodai Resolution marked the commencement of a struggle for the establishment of a separate state of Tamil Eelam. While there had been many demands for Tamil independence before, this resolution articulated, for the very first time, in very clear terms, the demand for an independent state for the Tamil nation based on their historical habitation of the northern and eastern provinces.[3] The Resolution came four years after the adoption of the 1972 Constitution. The 1972 Constitution made Sri Lanka a unitary state for the first time, gave 'foremost' place to Buddhism, and made Sinhala the official language. It also expressly precluded the courts from reviewing the constitutional validity of legislation and removed an important safeguard for minorities that was in the previous constitution. At around this time language based 'standardisation' with regard to entry to Sri Lankan universities had angered Tamil youth. The Vaddukodai Resolution and the

3 The Vaddukodai Resolution was adopted by the Tamil United Liberation Front (TULF) at its First National Convention of held at Vaddukoddai on 14th May 1976 under the chair of S.J.V. Chelvanayakam.

1972 Constitution are turning points in Sri Lankan politics. They resulted in the marginalisation of moderate forces and emergence of the radical forces among the Tamils of Sri Lanka.

Tamil groups began to embrace violence in the mid seventies. Over a period of time the LTTE emerged as the strongest group. In 1983 thirteen army soldiers were killed by the LTTE in Jaffna and soon after ethnic riots erupted in Colombo. Many Tamils were killed and many lost their property. Many left overseas in disgust and anger. There was substantial evidence to show that the state was involved in fuelling the riots or at the very least 'standing by' while the rioting and looting took place.

Since then the war was fought brutally by both government and LTTE. Both sides have attacked not only military targets but also civilians and their property, as well as other places including temples and places of historical and intellectual value. Over the years the UN Special Procedures and human rights groups have documented thousands of human rights violations by both the state and non-state actors.

The Muslims, many of whom have lived for many years in the East have suffered particularly. In 1990 about 70,000 Muslims were evicted overnight from the North by the LTTE and many have still not been able to return. During the conflict Muslim villages have been attacked and Muslim villagers butchered by the LTTE, who has accused Muslims of collaborating with Sri Lankan armed forces. Both Muslims and Tamils share the same language.

In January 2003 a group of students led by the student body of the South Eastern University adopted the Oluvil Declaration at a mass political rally held in Oluvil in the Ampara District of the Eastern Province. The Oluvil Declaration argued that the Muslims of the North East are a separate nationality and nation with a distinct identity, religion and culture. It noted that the North East is the traditional homeland of the Muslims and called for an autonomous, self-governing political unit linking all Muslim majority areas of the north and east (Muslim Thesam). It noted that Muslims must have separate representation at the then peace talks and that the final political settlement must have the consent of the Muslims.

Tamil groups had previously presented similar ideas in what is commonly known as the 'Thimpu Principles' and the Oluvil Declaration is in some respects a response to the Thimpu Principles. At the Peace Talks held in Thimpu, Bhutan in July 1985 six Tamil groups presented four cardinal principles which they said should shape any solution to the ethnic conflict:

1. Recognition of the Tamils as a distinct nationality.
2. Recognition of an identified Tamil homeland and the guarantee of its territorial integrity.
3. Based on the above, recognition of the inalienable right of self-determination of the Tamil nation.
4. Recognition of the right to full citizenship and other fundamental democratic rights of all Tamils, who look upon the island as their country.[4]

In the 1980s there was support for the militant Tamil groups from India and many of the armed groups received secret military training supported by the Research and Analysis Wing (RAW). The Indian support for the LTTE began to wane when a LTTE suicide bomber killed Prime Minister Rajiv Gandhi in the 1990s. In 1987 the Indian government persuaded the government of Sri Lanka and the LTTE to sign a peace accord and to agree to a quasi-federal state. Although the Sri Lankan government introduced the 13th and 16th Amendments to the Constitution and introduced a quasi-federal structure, the agreement collapsed and the war resumed.[5] For many years the LTTE had been in control of a portion of the North East of the country, mainly in the Jaffna, Mannar, Killinochchi, Mullativu and Vavuniya districts. In those regions it established rudimentary state structures including its own police force and a courts system. In LTTE controlled areas both free movement and free expression were subject to restrictions and any form of dissent tightly controlled.[6]

A new phase in the conflict commenced in 2006. After the LTTE launched a series of claymore mine attacks and attempted to kill the Army Commander and the Secretary Defence in suicide attacks, government forces launched a sustained military campaign to eliminate the LTTE. This culminated in the defeat of the LTTE as a military force in May 2009. Fighting alongside the government forces was a breakaway faction of the LTTE and other Tamil groups that had previously fought against the Sri Lankan state.

By the middle of 2007 government forces had taken control of the Eastern Province and in January 2009 wrested control of Killinochchi, the LTTE's administrative capital in the North. Soon after a major humanitarian crisis ensued with the

4 Statement made by a delegation of Tamil groups consisting of PLOTE, EPRLF, EROS, LTTE, TELO, and the TULF at the peace talks between the Government of Sri Lanka and Tamil groups held in Thimpu, Bhutan, July 1985. See *Tamil United Liberation Front*: Towards Devolution of Power in Sri Lanka. Main Documents, Madras 1988, p. 17, also commonly known as the 'Thimpu Principles'. See also *Ketheeshwaran Loganathan*: Sri Lanka. Lost Opportunities: Past Attempts at Resolving Ethnic Conflict, Colombo 1996.

5 Indo-Sri Lanka Agreement to Establish Peace and Normalcy in Sri Lanka, 29th July 1987.

6 See also *Jayadeva Uyangoda*: Ethnic Conflict in Sri Lanka: Changing Dynamics, Washington D.C. 2007.

LTTE holding thousands of Tamil civilians hostage and the government repeatedly shelling LTTE controlled areas, including civilian targets. UN officials estimated that about 7,500 were killed and about 15,000 wounded between January and early May 2009, when the LTTE and the government fought the final battles. Many more are thought to have died between early May and the 19th May when the government announced the elimination of most of the LTTE leadership.

The 2002-2003 Peace Process

There have been many attempts to negotiate a peace in Sri Lanka, the most serious of which was in 2002-2003. The United National Front government was elected to power in December 2001 and the LTTE declared a unilateral ceasefire on Christmas Eve of that year. The government responded and the two parties signed a Norwegian-brokered ceasefire agreement in February 2002. After a year of unexpected progress and six rounds of talks in Thailand, Norway, Japan and Germany, the process stopped as suddenly as it started.

The Ceasefire Agreement of 2002 was based on an acceptance of the then-military balance of power, which meant an acceptance by the Sri Lankan state that the LTTE controlled certain areas of territory and the recognition of those forward defence lines as well as an equal parity of status for the LTTE. The Ceasefire Agreement also emphasised the urgency of restoring a sense of normalcy in the North of the country and an opening of the only land route – the A9 highway – between the North and South. It ensured that Norway would continue as mediator and established the Sri Lanka Monitoring Mission (SLMM) consisting of Scandinavian monitors led by Norway and local monitoring teams, to monitor the ceasefire.

The Tsunami of 2004

The tsunami of 26th December 2004 killed over 30,000 people and destroyed livelihoods and property on an unprecedented scale. It devastated coastlines on the north, east, south and west coasts of Sri Lanka and shattered the hopes and aspirations of people from all communities. Many of those who suffered from the tsunami had already suffered as a result of the conflict. While the scale of the tsunami was unprecedented, the wave of human solidarity it generated was similarly unparalleled. It mobilised Sri Lankans and non-Sri Lankans, both within and outside the country on an unprecedented scale. Many from all around the world were moved to pledge large sums of money for reconstruction and rebuilding. Others were moved to visit and participate physically in the reconstruction and rebuilding process. Governments from all parts of the world also responded magnificently with generous pledges of humanitarian aid and other assistance.

At the time the tsunami struck there was some apprehension that the ceasefire would not hold for much longer. Soon after the tsunami and in the light of the destruction caused to the northern and eastern regions of the country, some foresaw that the wave of the destruction had opened a window of opportunity to revive and nourish a stagnant peace process. In January 2005 there was hope that the disaster would provide a catalyst to reestablishing trust between the government and the LTTE on the one hand and between the LTTE and the Muslim community on the other. The disaster provided an opportunity for the government and the LTTE to collaborate on rebuilding and reconstruction after the tsunami. It was an opportunity to look at the creation of new arrangements and structures in matters pertaining to post-tsunami rebuilding and reconstruction in the hopes that these initial arrangements would metamorphose into something more permanent for the North and East. Yet this did not materialise in any anticipated way. The LTTE and the government began discussions on a joint post-tsunami aid mechanism but this process was shattered by the assassination of a senior LTTE leader in February 2005. Negotiations resumed through the facilitation of the Norwegian government, and then in late June 2005 the government and the LTTE signed the Post Tsunami Operational Management Structure (P-TOMS) Agreement. This agreement envisaged the establishment of a three-tiered system that would involve the government, the LTTE and the Muslims in the supervision and implementation of post-tsunami rebuilding activities. It was the first time that the LTTE had entered into an agreement with the government on a matter pertaining to governance.

The P-TOMS Agreement drew considerable criticism from most sections of the Muslim community. Muslims, especially those in the eastern coastal regions, suffered significantly as a result of the tsunami and the Muslims were angered because of their exclusion from the process of negotiations and also because of the role that was assigned to them in the P-TOMS structure. The agreement was challenged by members of the Janatha Vimukthi Peramuna (JVP) before the Supreme Court and the Court stayed parts of the agreement in an Interim Order given in July.[7] The agreement has not been revived since.

Framing a New Constitutional Settlement

A 2005 Report on Human Security argues that about 60 dictatorships have collapsed, that the number of wars has decreased and that the number of democracies has increased in the last 30 years.[8]

Sri Lanka faces a number of challenges at the current moment. These include:

7 Wimal Weerawansa v Attorney General, Supreme Court Minutes of 15th July 2005 (Interim Order of the Court).

8 *University of British Columbia, Human Security Centre*: Human Security Report 2005. War and Peace in the 21st Century, New York 2005.

1. Responding to the humanitarian crisis and restoring the damaged infrastructure in the North East to create conditions of normalcy as quickly as possible.
2. Initiating processes of reconciliation and healing among all communities.
3. Evolving a power sharing agreement that will accommodate the aspirations of the Sinhalese, Tamils and Muslims and ensure equality for all.
4. Restoring the rule of law and ensuring the re-establishment of effective, independent and credible institutions.

One of the fundamental challenges the country faces is the transformation of the Sri Lankan state. If Sri Lanka is to ensure that there is a sustained peace and no return to war then there can be no return to the old order of the state. There needs to be a new state that recognises the multiethnic and plural nature of Sri Lankan society and gives priority to the rule of law. The new state will need to entrench a system of power sharing between the centre and the regions which is constitutionally protected and not easily alterable. This will need to be supported by a strong Bill of Rights with strong guarantees of individual and group equality, credible institutions, and effective legal remedies for all communities.

A constitutional settlement for Sri Lanka should contain the following elements if there is to be an enduring transition:

- Recognise the multiethnic, multireligious and multilingual character of Sri Lankan society and provide ways for fostering this diversity.
- Ensure that no community enjoys privileges or benefits not enjoyed by other communities. Similarly, no community should suffer any disadvantage not imposed on the other communities.
- Establish a united state which protects and promotes the diversity of all peoples.
- Provide for effective autonomy and power sharing between the centre and the regions.
- Protect the right to self-determination of any of Sri Lanka's constituent peoples, whether founded on a commonality of language, culture, religion or territory within the framework of a united state.
- Ensure that men and women enjoy equal rights in law and in practice.
- Provide for the supremacy of the constitution at all times.
- Provide for all laws, regulations and policy to be in accordance with international human rights.

- Establish a constitutional court consisting of experts in the subject to interpret the constitution and resolve disputes between the centre and the regions, and between regions.
- Provide for multiparty democracy and ensure the accountability and transparency of all institutions of governance.
- Provide that national institutions reflect the diversity of the people and communities and have equitable representation from both sexes.
- Provide for a second chamber of parliament to facilitate power sharing at the centre. The second chamber should consist of representatives from all regions and from all the communities.
- Provide for a culture of multilingualism and the effective implementation of all three languages: Sinhala, Tamil and English.
- Provide for independent commissions to support democracy, increase transparency and promote human rights which will include a:

  Human Rights Commission,

  Gender Equality Commission,

  Ethics and Integrity Commission,

  Finance Commission, and

  Elections Commission.

Restoring the Rule of Law

Among the challenges the country faces is the task of restoring the rule of law. Restoring the rule of law means at the very least ensuring that people are made accountable for their crimes, including their past crimes, and that victims are provided with compensation and reparation. It will also require re-establishing the independence and credibility of Sri Lanka's public institutions. At the moment, there is no institution that commands the credibility and confidence of the Sri Lankan public. Ensuring the independence and effectiveness of the police, which is responsible for investigating crimes; the Attorney-General's department, which is responsible for prosecuting crimes; and the Human Rights Commission, which has a broad mandate to protect and promote human rights, is a priority. In the recent past, Sri Lanka has established a number of institutions, which include the Constitutional Council, the Human Rights Commission, the Police Commission, the Public Service Commission, the Commission to Investigate All Forms of Bribery and Corruption, and the Elections Commission, none of which had a major impact on public life in the country.

Restoring the rule of law will also mean that the extraordinary legal powers vested in the armed forces and police by emergency regulations and the Prevention of Terrorism Act should be removed. Emergency regulations issued by the executive under the Public Security Ordinance, and the Prevention of Terrorism Act of 1979, have given the armed forces and police extraordinary powers to arrest, interrogate and detain people on a mere suspicion and for extended periods of time, with limited judicial supervision and scrutiny.

Other powers have enabled the disposal of bodies without a post-mortem, the establishment of 'high security zones', and the establishment of centres of detention in almost any part of the country. A comprehensive register with the names and locations of all those under detention has never been available. The country has been governed by emergency regulations for the most part of the last forty years. Very few emergency regulations have been struck down by the courts for their unconstitutionality.

Restoring the rule of law would require that there be judicial supervision and scrutiny of the declaration of an emergency; the continued 'use' of an emergency; and the constitutionality of emergency regulations. Giving the courts the power to review the constitutional validity of laws, taken away by the 1972 and 1978 constitutions, is of paramount importance. Ensuring that judicial appointments are de-politicised and that promotions within the judiciary are based on merit and seniority will help re-establish the independence of that organ of government. Restoring the rule of law will also require that the state passes legislation criminalising enforced disappearances in accordance with the International Convention for the Protection of All Persons from Enforced Disappearance. Disappearances caused by non-state actors should also be criminalised.

The Role of the International Community

Sri Lankans will have to take on the bulk of the responsibility for creating a lasting peace. A constitutional peace is more likely to endure where there is local ownership of the process and where all local stakeholders participate. While local stakeholders will have to take primary responsibility, the international community can also facilitate this process by taking a principled stance on some fundamental issues. The international community has traditionally included only governments. However, it is important to broaden this concept to include international civil society and international business.

The international community has at least five important roles to play in this post-conflict stage:

- As a persistent advocate of a political settlement to the conflict based on equality for all communities; a respect for human rights; and a re-establishment of the rule of law.
- As experts assisting in the framing of a new constitution.
- As experts in a process of post-conflict justice exploring and responding to past human rights violations.
- As donors funding reconstruction, development, peace, and human rights work.
- As investors who encourage private investment.

The current Sri Lankan regime has proven itself immune to international criticism in some cases, and has demonstrated a capacity to manage international criticism in others. The international community should consider linking up with international civil society organisations and the international business sector to support and nourish those civil society organisations and those parts of the business sector within Sri Lanka that continue to push for a new constitutional settlement; respect for human rights; and respect for the rule of law. Within Sri Lanka, the business sector has a lot of potential as a driver of peaceful change, most of which remains unexploited.

One of the benefits of globalisation is today's vision of a global normative order that tells us that the rights of all persons everywhere are the concern of all states and governments. Where a state is unwilling to address the root causes of internal conflict and respond to compelling human needs, the international community has a responsibility to act.[9] The international community has a responsibility to continue to engage in the internal conflict in Sri Lanka even if its impact has so far been limited.

The current moment provides a unique opportunity for the Sri Lankan state to build a sustainable peace and create the building blocks for a plural and caring society. It will require the courage to take some hard decisions, the imagination to dream anew and the humility to reach out to all those who suffered during the conflict. Inept political leadership and an indifferent civil society have seen the country squander many opportunities in the past. Events since the end of the war in 2009 suggest that this important moment will slip by yet again and another opportunity will be squandered.

9 See the Report of the *International Commission on Intervention and State Sovereignty*: The Responsibility to Protect, Ottawa 2001, on when coercive action may be appropriate to protect people at risk in another state.

References

Edrisinha, Rohan/Gomez, Mario/Thamilmaran, V.T./Welikala, Asanga: Power Sharing in Sri Lanka: Constitutional and Political Documents 1926-2008 (Berghof Foundation for Conflict Studies and the Centre for Policy Alternatives), Colombo 2008

International Commission on Intervention and State Sovereignty: The Responsibility to Protect, Ottawa 2001

International Crisis Group: Sri Lanka's Human Rights Crisis. Asia Report No. 135, 14. 06. 2007; http://www.crisisgroup.org/en/regions/asia/south-asia/sri-lanka/135-sri-lankas-human-rights-crisis.aspx [15. 10. 2010]

Lederach, John Paul: The Moral Imagination. The Art and Soul of Building Peace, New York 2005

Loganathan, Ketheeshwaran: Sri Lanka. Lost Opportunities: Past Attempts at Resolving Ethnic Conflict, Colombo 1996

Tamil United Liberation Front: Towards Devolution of Power in Sri Lanka. Main Documents, Madras 1988

University of British Columbia, Human Security Centre: Human Security Report 2005. War and Peace in the 21st Century, New York 2005

Uyangoda, Jayadeva: Ethnic Conflict in Sri Lanka. Changing Dynamics, Washington D.C. 2007

Intercultural Dialogue Between European and Non-European Societies in a Globalised World

Mona Abousenna

The first part of this paper tackles two interrelated issues: globalisation and intercultural dialogue. I will start by defining the concept of globalisation as it is used in this paper. I will then relate it to intercultural dialogue. Within this context, I use my own definition of globalisation as the frame of reference against which the two issues will be presented and discussed. First: what do I mean by globalisation?

Linguistically, globalisation derives from the Greek word 'globus' meaning planet earth. The term, thus, refers to the globe as a single unit where all kinds of barriers have fallen, including those of time and space, due to the scientific and technological revolution. Hence, globalisation is the outcome of the scientific and technological revolution which has produced an unprecedented revolution in the fields of knowledge and information to the extent that Peter Drucker, in his famous book *The New Realities*, has coined the term 'knowledge society'[1] to refer to the age in which we live today. This new interconnected universe is creating a global consciousness that supersedes the old, fragmented world of separate and closed cultural identities.

My own understanding of globalisation runs counter to the current and popular understanding of the term which restricts it to the political and economic spheres. This narrowing of the term offers an analysis of globalisation, which is a 21st century phenomenon, by relying upon experiences of the 19th and early 20th century that have been superseded by the phenomenon of globalisation in every aspect, and particularly with regards to the nature of regional and global conflicts and the ways and means of their resolution. Examples of global phenomena that call for global solutions are: global terrorism, global trade, global environmental issues, global pandemic disease, among many others. Second: what do I mean by intercultural dialogue? But, first, what is dialogue?

The etymology of the word 'dialogue' derives from the Greek *dialogos* and *dialogomai*, which mean to converse. Dialogue is different from debate, wherein each party present their own views without regard to the views of the other. In dialogue, each party must listen to the other as openly and as sympathetically as possible in an attempt to understand the other's position as precisely and as much from within as possible.

1 *Drucker, Peter F.*: The New Realities, London 1989.

In the cultural sense, dialogue, or more precisely dialogue of cultures, could be defined as communication on a common subject among two or more parties, individuals or groups, with differing views or with common views, the purpose of which is for each partner to learn from the other so that each can grow and change. Such an attitude includes the assumption that at any point we might find the partner's position and arguments so persuasive that we could change. In this sense, change could be radical.

Cultures enter into dialogue so that they can learn, change and grow, not so that they can force change on other cultures, as in the case of debate. Moreover, dialogue can only take place between equals, which means that there can be no such thing as one-way dialogue. In the absence of equality, there can be a gathering of data in the manner of a questionnaire or an interrogation. Dialogue can take place only on the basis of mutual trust. Individuals entering into dialogue must be at least minimally self-critical of both themselves and their own cultural traditions, especially those that hinder dialogue. A lack of such self-criticism implies that one's own tradition already has all the correct answers and is tantamount to an absolute. Such an attitude makes dialogue not only unnecessary, but even impossible, since we enter into dialogue primarily in order to learn, which obviously cannot be the case if one sees one's own tradition as absolutely infallible. Such attitude hinders the partners' attempt to experience each other's cultures from within.

Intercultural dialogue is a step beyond cultural dialogue because it must be built upon the preconditions demanded by dialogue of cultures, without which it could not happen. If the target of cultural dialogue is change, which could be radical, intercultural dialogue necessitates this radical change. It allows the dialogists to intervene and interfere in each other's fundamental beliefs and criticise them radically with the purpose of eliminating conflict and establishing a real dialogue that leads to peaceful relations between cultures. Like a dialogue of cultures, intercultural dialogue means establishing cultural communication via a common frame of reference. By a common frame of reference I mean a specific perspective that regards human civilisation within a historical course evolving from mythos to logos, thus uniting civilisation and, at the same time, indicating diversity of cultures within the same civilisational process. The oneness of civilisation and the diversity of cultures represents he common denominator of cultural dialogue. In this sense, diversity of cultures, which stresses differences and conflicts between cultures, will be managed by the commonalities and oneness of human civilisation and directed towards partnership and peaceful interdependence.

This brings us to the second part of my paper which raised two related questions: First: what are the obstacles that stand in the way of a genuine intercultural dialogue between European and non-European societies? Second: what are the possible solutions to these obstacles?

In answer to the first question, I think that the major obstacle is represented by the global phenomenon of Islamic Fundamentalism, as distinct from all other forms of religious fundamentalisms, because it aims at Islamising the entire globe. In this sense, violence, in its minimum level, and terrorism, as the maximum, is indigenous to the ideology of Islamic fundamentalism. I will elaborate from the writings of the founders of the movements of the Brotherhood which emerged in Egypt in 1928 and spread across the world.

In his famous book titled *Landmarks* – or in some translations *Milestones* – Qutb reduces Islam to the Quran. He writes: "The first fountain source from which the first generation drew upon was the Quran, and the Quran only, as the Prophet's hadith is just an outcome of that source."[2]

He, then, goes on to explain his own understanding of Islam:

> "Islam is not just a faith (*a'keeda*). Islam is a universal declaration for the liberation of Man from slavery to men. Its main goal is to eliminate the regimes and governments which are founded on the governance of humans and the slavery of people to people."[3]

According to Qutb, religion or *deen* is much broader than faith or *akeeda*. He writes: "Religion is the method and the system which controls life. Although it is founded on faith, it is much broader and more comprehensive."[4]

By that, Qutb means that religion, which to him is Islam, encompasses the whole of human life from politics to private personal affairs. Religion thus becomes the imperative of establishing what he calls *hakimiyya* or the rule of Allah within human society by applying the divine laws of *shari'a*, which "is the only form of liberating human beings totally from slavery to each other... (and) this is the 'human civilisation'."[5] In answer to the question, how can this be realised?, Qutb replies: "by *jihad*." In a chapter titled *Jihad for Allah*, he describes *jihad* as "an Islamic activist movement which uses the sword beside the word," and he adds,

> "*jihad* has never been, and can never be a defensive movement in the narrow sense understood by the present-day term 'defensive war'. Islam has been a movement forward to liberate man on earth by means compatible with reality, using the instruments appropriate to every stage."[6]

It appears quite clear from the above quotations that faith, which is an integral part of religion according to Qutb, is essentially and intrinsically related to the use of violence, applying the appropriate instruments as a means to wage the holy offen-

2 *Sayyid Qutb*: Milestones, Cairo 1964, p. 15.
3 Ibid., p. 71.
4 Ibid.
5 Ibid., p. 118.
6 Ibid., p. 72.

sive war of *jihad* with the purpose of imposing Islam on the entire world. (This is not very different from the concept of martyrdom within Shiite Islam, as outlined by Ali Shariati, the theoretician of the Iranian Islamic Revolution in his book *On the Sociology of Islam.*[7]) Against the background of these ideas of Qutb, the Muslim Brotherhood movement, or *Hizb al-Ikhwan al-Muslimun*, was founded by Hassan el-Banna in Egypt under the motto: "Allah is our objective. The Prophet is our leader. The Quran is our law. *Jihad* is our way. Dying on the path of Allah is our highest hope."

Since then, the movement has profoundly influenced the political life of the Middle East. But the Middle East is only one part of the Muslim world which the movement has targeted. With the emergence of the phenomenon of globalisation, accompanied by the phenomenon of terrorism, at the close of the 20th century and the rise of the 21st, it was becoming increasingly evident that the four decades of organised political teaching and military activism by the Brotherhood movement have had their impact in all parts of the world, and in particular within Europe. Hence, Europe has become an incubator for their thought and political development. Since the 1960s, Muslim Brotherhood members and sympathisers have moved to Europe and slowly but steadily established a wide and well-grounded network of mosques, charities and Islamic organisations. Unlike the larger Islamic community, the Brotherhood's ultimate goal has been to extend Islamic law throughout Europe and the United States.

Based on the above-mentioned knowledge, we could then raise the following questions:

- Is intercultural dialogue possible or impossible in light of global Islamic fundamentalism and terrorism?
- What are the historical causes for the emergence of this phenomenon, both within the European and the Arab and Muslim contexts?
- In an age of post-colonialism, how can we re-evaluate the phenomenon of colonialism in light of present-day Islamic fundamentalism and terrorism?
- Is it possible to develop a philosophy, or philosophies, of globalisation that could clarify the phenomenon of Islamic fundamentalism and terrorism in light of globalisation?

It is up to the Karlsruhe Dialogues project and to ZAK to respond to these questions in the forthcoming conferences.

---

7 *Shariati, Ali*: On the Sociology of Islam, Berkeley 1979.

To conclude, I would like to add that the 11th conference of the Karlsruhe Dialogues presents a positive model to be emulated by similar projects, namely, to look at Europe and its future from non-European views. In order to proceed forward in this direction, I would like to recommend the following:

First, we should aim at building a common future of European and non-European societies, particularly Arab and Islamic societies. To do so, we should not dwell upon the burdens of the past, but rather address the unsolved problems of the new world order of globalisation in order to construct new patterns of mutual understanding and cooperation.

Second, Arabs and Muslims should be seen as one of the major factors that will shape the future of Europe. Thus, the extrapolation of Europe's future by the Arab and Islamic world is a very important issue to Europe's fate.

Third, we should look out for bridges of intercultural communication, which means mediating between two different cultural frames of reference for the sake of pushing both cultural identities towards true development that might fit into globalisation.

Fourth, we should avoid falling into the illusion that technology can be a bridge between the West and the Islamic world because technology is transported without its inherent value system, a system which represents modernity and enlightened values.

Cultures in Conflict or in Dialogue? Europe in the 21st Century Seen from Egypt

Mourad Wahba

The title of this paper refers to two conferences that were held in Egypt: the first one was on the theme 'Cultures in Conflict or in Dialogue?' (November 1991). The conference was initiated by Cardinal Poupard, Head of the Pontifical Council for Culture at the Vatican, who presented a proposal to the Afro-Asian Philosophy Association (AAPA, an international philosophy association affiliated to the International Federation of Philosophical Societies (FISP) which I was presiding at the time) to hold a joint conference on the above-mentioned theme.

Culture has been and still is *the* major issue that has concerned the AAPA since its inception in 1978, when it held its first international conference in Cairo on the theme 'Philosophy and Civilisation'. The main objective of the association is to bridge the civilisational gap between developed and developing countries. This gap was a result of the absence (among developing countries) of two phases which were undergone by developed countries, namely the sovereignty of reason and the commitment of reason to change reality for the benefit of the people. These two phases were initiated in Europe by two historical movements, the Reformation in the 16th century and the Enlightenment in the 18th century. The first movement advocated the liberation of reason from religious authority while the second called for the sovereignty of reason in all fields. That is, both movements called for the freedom of human reason, one within religious matters and the other within all fields of society and knowledge.

However, after the first Gulf War, the AAPA observed the emerging conflict between the Islamic world and the West or, more precisely, Western culture. Thus, we decided to establish another association to address the newly emerging issues and problematics arising from this immanent global cultural threat. The new association adopted the ideas of the medieval Muslim philosopher Averroes (Ibn Rushd) as a bridge between the two cultures. The rationale for choosing this philosopher, rather than anybody else, is the fact that he, more than any other Muslim philosopher, was the forerunner of those two historical movements which are absent in the Islamic world, namely religious reformation and enlightenment. The essence of Averroes's philosophy is 'interpretation' which necessitates the use of logical and demonstrative reasoning in order to reveal the hidden meaning or, more precisely, the metaphorical meaning of the religious text. Because of his advocating for interpretation of religious texts, Averroes was charged with atheism, his books were burnt and he was exiled. He therefore became marginal in the history of Islamic culture, whereas in Europe his ideas were instrumental in creating the trend of Latin Averroism which spread all over the continent.

As for the second conference, to which the second part of this paper's title refers, it was held in Cairo on the theme 'Europe's Future in the Arab View' in February 1981, and was jointly organised by the Middle East Research Center at Ain Shams University and the Institute of International Relations in Bonn. At that conference, I presented a paper entitled 'The Future of the Arabs without Europe'. This title was formulated according to my view that the civilisational gap between Europe and the Islamic world is due to a long history of hatred and the latter's cultural isolation from the West, to the extent that whenever Islamic thinkers in the Islamic world have declared that they were influenced by the ideas of Western thinkers, they were persecuted and accused of atheism and blasphemy.

Now, within the context of those two conferences, let me illustrate how Europe is seen from an Egyptian perspective.

Egypt, today, is controlled by both Islamic and Christian fundamentalists because secularisation as a term and as a way of life is a cultural taboo, whereas Europe's main trend, on the contrary, is not religious fundamentalism but secularisation. Hence, Europe is seen as an a mainly atheistic culture. That is why the movement of Muslim Brotherhood is prevailing in Egypt and will continue to prevail unless a secular trend emerges to counteract and weaken the fundamentalist trend. The Islamic fundamentalist trend is viewed as a negative force against Western culture and towards any futuristic outlook on the ground that the locus of the golden age was in the past and not in the future. Even those who advocate the spirit of modernism are somewhat abortive, and if this abortive attitude is viewed as a positive attitude towards the West it is at the same time tradition-bound. It is not much more than enlightened traditionalism and that is why this abortive modernism ultimately and fundamentally opposes secular elements of social modernisation more effectively that tradionalism.

The two most influential figures in the tradionalist movement were Jamal-al-Din Afghani and Mohamad Abdou. It must be stressed from the outset that this movement, spearheaded by these two Muslim thinkers, did not question the Muslim dogma. Its primary impulse lay in the challenges which Europe posed to Egypt. Its aim was to reinstitute and strengthen religious dogma, not to expose it to rational criticism. Thus, Abdou gave this trend its promissory formulation, and the task he set himself involved two things: first, a restatement of what Islam really is; second, a consideration of its implications for modern society. As for the first point, Abdou is of the opinion that reason must accept everything that is in the Koran without hesitation: once it is acknowledged that Muhammad is Allah's prophet, the entire content of his message must be accepted. The second point proceeds from the first, for as long as reason is controlled by the Koran, so the ideal society is that which submits to Allah commandments, for these commandments are also the principles of human society. The behaviour which the Koran teaches is also that which modern social thought views as the key to progress. Islam is the true sociology, the science of happiness in this world as well as in the next. So, when Islamic law is fully obeyed society flourishes, and when it is rejected society decays.

Thus, we can conclude that in order for Egypt to go into dialogue with the West in the 21st century, Europe should encourage the intellectual space that breeds secularisation and enlightenment. If this happens, dialogue could emerge and push forward enlightened ideas so that, in time, the two partners may fight the fundamentalist trend hand in hand.

"The Individual Is Always Defeated in the End"

Michael March

For Jean Genet, "the master determines the definition of words." Criminals remain hidden – drinks are served.

If language speaks, it speaks to those that know. For Kazantzakis, "the devil has blue eyes and red hair." For Gombrowicz, "the forest is green." For Brecht, Socrates "didn't believe in the gods, he believed in onions."

In this business of living, "we must *necessarily* misunderstand ourselves." We build upon the dead – "the dead are gentle to us" – "life is a dance on graves" – we remain "condemned to hope."

In this business of living, "the natural state of man is war" – war "the destruction of good restaurants."

We live in a police state – where nihilists don't believe their eyes. Kazantzakis wished to change the eyes that see reality. Better to adopt – "a delicacy of heart."

If we define Europe as "the landmass behind Greece" – we see what we already know – everything can be destroyed – except myth.

"My brothers were cruel – I am the cruelest – and it is *I* who weep at night."

We have needs that "cannot be satisfied by any rational means – the gravest human disorders cannot be remedied, only treated day by day."

"In the beginning the wound is invisible."

*

When Primo Levi returned to Turin, he wrote: "I come from very far away to bring you bad news" – "all of us human seed, we live and die for nothing" – "the skies perpetually revolve in vain."

We build upon each other – live *against* each other.

*

The Greeks used the word diagnosis: "to recognise – to know." Aeschylus saw us "suffering into truth" – a performance – mysterious, insufficient – insufferable.

Assume "loss precedes presence" – "beauty difficult" – our chains – almost divine.

Assume the invisible subsumes the visible – culture – "the formation of recognition" – man a *potential* being.

*

I came to Europe from New York – an eternal city – an incidental city – blue alligator sewers – black, vernacular subways – rosaries of discordant, evasive light – "when one day, in the compartment of some train, as I was looking at the passenger sitting across from me, I was suddenly struck by the realisation that any man *is worth* any other. Behind what was visible of this man – I discovered – a kind of identity common to all men."

All cultures remain provincial – protective – almost tribal – all truths in fluctuation – "at last I was free either to sleep or to fly – instead, I decided to put on one sock."

*

"Ill at ease in the tyranny – ill at ease in the republic – in the one I longed for freedom – in the other the end of corruption."

"Spinoza understood that humans are an integral part of the natural world, so he never turned to the state for salvation. States are at the mercy of events as much as any human institution, and over the long course of history all of them fail."

"The real enemy of man is History."

*

The European Union transmits the past – not *necessarily* a bad choice – if in maintaining peace – it realises that "any country can achieve democracy – and any can lose it."

For those looking in – "the attempt to project democracy beyond the national level has failed." For those in the dark – "terrible is the temptation for goodness" – "they know, yet they do."

*

"States are bound to rank their vital interests over more universal considerations. This involves giving priority to their citizens. Because they first must serve the interests of who they rule, states cannot adopt an impartial perspective – often thought to be essential to morality – but that does not mean their policies cannot be judged morally."

"At its best, politics is not a vehicle for universal projects but the art of responding to the flux of circumstances."

*

For Marx, "the world is a warehouse of commodities, a place of total availability and exchange" – man becomes "the most important raw material – to be used and exploited."

For Flaubert, "life seems bearable, when one succeeds in avoiding it."

"Man forms himself only as a fragment" – held together by "the universal glue of stupidity."

"Nothing is as vast as emptiness."

*

"Art is magic liberated from the lie of being truth."

"Through the distance of time, literature preserves beauty – which, in turn, saves our world."

For those looking away – our age mimics Marcus Aurelius – "discard your thirst for books – so that you won't die in bitterness."

For Napoleon, "war is a simple art based entirely on execution."

*

In *Brave New World* – "the optimum population is modeled on the iceberg – eight-ninths below the water line, one-ninth above" – those in the dark remain hidden – "truth is a menace."

In Brussels – "The Europe of Tomorrow will be the result of three liberations – the liberation after the Second World War, the liberation from the Cold War, and the liberation from the fear of foreigners and their eventual total integration into a new Europe."

"Whoever's laughing hasn't heard the latest news."

*

Joseph Roth wrote, "I can die for the masses – but not live with them."

NATO and the European Union have drawn the same conclusion – "a pre-emptive nuclear strike – as a key option" – warning us of "environmental migration on a mass scale."

"In the beginning the wound is invisible."

Search for "a delicacy of heart."

*

As for integration – we perceive an unrequited union – a cobblestone empire – whose "blood spurts from the scab of stock phrases" – whose expansion "does violence to the truth." Not quite the art of acquiescence – but the vanity of empire – expanding – "slaves learning slavery" – "bleached bones in fields of yellow sand."

*

Susan Sontag observed: "We live in a time which is experienced as the end – more exactly, just past the end – of every ideal, and therefore of culture – there is no possibility of true culture without altruism."

We reply, "culture is the formation of recognition" – let the man go free.

About the Authors

Dr. Tahir Abbas was born and brought up in Birmingham, whereas his father comes from Kashmir/Pakistan. Migration and the Muslim minority are topics that became central aspects within his professional life. Abbas took an economics degree from Queen Mary, London, completed his Master of Social Science in economic development and policy at the University of Birmingham and he received his Ph.D. in ethnic relations at the University of Warwick. Afterwards, Abbas was an ESRC research fellow at the University of Central England Business School. In addition, he worked as a Senior Research Officer at the Home Office and the Department for Constitutional Affairs in London and as project director of race equality in Worcester. Abbas is formerly founding director of the Centre for the Study of Ethnicity and Culture at the University of Birmingham, where he taught sociology. He is currently head of research, policy and international relations at the DEEN Foundation – a community interest charity which aims to build models of economic success to counter ethnic and religious conflict in developed and developing worlds. Education, integration, multiculturalism and the radicalisation of young people from Britain and Western Europe, who belong to Muslim minorities, are topics Abbas deals with also in his publications. In doing so, he for instance refers to the terror attacks in London in the year 2005, which were committed by British Muslims. The cause and reasons for this radicalisation should be found, as Abbas said in an article published on *NZZ Online* in 2005, in social and economic circumstances.

Publications i. a.:

Islamic Radicalism and Multicultural Politics. The British Experience, London/ New York 2010

(ed.): Islamic Political Radicalism: A European Perspective, Edinburgh 2007

(ed.): Muslim Britain. Communities under Pressure, New York 2005

Prof. Dr. Mona Abousenna was born in Cairo/Egypt in 1945. She studied English literature, received her B.A. at Cairo University in 1967 and her M.A. at Ain Shams University in 1977. There, she also completed her Ph.D. in the year 1980. Since 1968, Abousenna has been working at the English Department, Faculty of Education at Ain Shams University as lecturer, assistant professor, and then in 1991 she was appointed professor of English literature. At the same university she additionally covered a number of administrative duties: Most recently she has been head of the English department from 1992 to 2000. Between 1990 and 2000 she has been director of the Center for Developing English Language Teaching (CDELT). Since 1990 she is a member of the Translation Committee at the Egyptian Supreme Council for Culture. In addition, Abousenna is a member of several international institutions: She serves as secretary general to the Afro-Asian Philosophy Association (AAPA) and to the Averroes and Enlightenment International Association, both of which she founded together with Mourad Wahba.

Publications i. a.:

Together with *Mourad Wahba* (eds.): Fundamentalism and Secularization in the Middle East, Cairo 1998

Together with *Mourad Wahba* (eds.): Religion and the Modernization of Cultures, Washington D.C. 1995

Prof. Dr. Nasr H. Abu Zaid was born in Egypt in 1943. After he completed his Arabic and Islamic studies he received his Ph.D. at Cairo University with Highest Honours in the year 1981. Abu Zaid could look back on a long career at University. From 1972 to 1995 he worked at the Department of Arabic Language and Literature at Cairo University, by the end as a professor. As a result of his critical interpretation of the Koran, his marriage was declared null and avoid on the basis of the Hishab and Abu Zaid received several threats on his life. These circumstances forced him to go into exile to Holland in 1995. In the same year, he was appointed in Leiden University as a visiting professor for Islamic studies. In addition, he worked in the project 'Rights at Home' at the International Institute for the Study of Islam in the Modern Muslim World (ISIM) from 2001 to 2004. Since 2002 Abu Zaid had the Ibn Rushd Chair of Islam and Humanism at the University of Humanistics in Utrecht/Netherlands. First and foremost, Abu Zaid dealt with Islamic theology, philosophy and politics as well as with Islam and humanism. Hermeneutics was his main topic of research and in this context he worked on the question of how Muslim people can connect their own tradition with the modern world. He wrote and published several books and papers and has received a great number of awards and prizes, among others the Roosevelt Institute Medal for Freedom of Worship (2002), the Ibn Rushd Prize for Freedom of Thought (2005) and the Prize for Freedom of Thought by the Muslim Democrats Society in Denmark (2006). He died in July 2010 in Cairo.

Publications i. a.:

Together with *Hilal Sezgin*: Mohammed und die Zeichen Gottes. Der Koran und die Zukunft des Islam, Freiburg im Breisgau 2008

Gottes Menschenwort. Für ein humanistisches Verständnis des Koran, Georges Anawati Stiftung No. 3, ed. by Thomas Hildebrandt, Freiburg im Breisgau 2008

Islam, Muslims and the West. Religion and Secularism. From Polarization to Negotiation, in: Islam and Europe. Challenges and Opportunities, Leuven 2008, pp. 113-125

Rethinking the Qur'an. Towards a Humanistic Hermeneutics, Utrecht 2004

Ein Leben mit dem Islam, ed. by Navid Kermani, Freiburg im Breisgau 1999

Prof. Dr. Anil Bhatti was born in 1944 and studied german studies, political sciences and philosophy. He received his Ph.D. at the University of Munich/Germany in 1971. In the same year, he started to work at the Centre of German Studies, School of Languages, Literature and Culture Studies at Jawaharlal Nehru University in New Delhi/India, where in 1983 he was appointed professor. He has been repeatedly chairperson of the Centre and has served a term as dean of the school. Additionally, he was chief editor of the *Journal of the School of Languages* between 1974 and 1984. His vast knowledge about German literature in the 20th century brought him to Kassel and Tübingen/Germany as well as to Graz and Vienna/ Austria where he lectured as a visiting professor. Bhatti was member of the International Advisory Committee of the International Association for Germanic Studies (IVG) and of the Indo-German Consultative Group. From 1996 to 2001, he was President of the Research Institute for Austrian and International Literature and Cultural Studies (INST) in Vienna. Bhatti was repeatedly research fellow of the Alexander von Humboldt Foundation: The first time between 1975 and 1976, then in 1982 and 1983 and in 2004 again. Today Bhatti is President of the Goethe Society of India. Bhatti is recipient of the Jacob- und Wilhelm-Grimm-Prize donated by the DAAD in 2001 and the Officer's Cross of the Order of Merit of the Federal Republic of Germany in 2005. Bhatti's main interest lies on German literature of the 19th and 20th Century, comparative literature and the theory of literature as well as on comparative culture studies between Europe and India/Asia. He has published many articles on these subjects and is co-editor of several books.

Publications i. a.:

Information and Security. Where Truth Lies, New Delhi 2008

Together with *Horst Turk* (eds.): Reisen, Entdecken, Utopien. Untersuchungen zum Alteritätsdiskurs im Kontext von Kolonialismus und Kulturkritik, Bern 1998

Together with *Horst Turk* (eds.): Kulturelle Identität. Deutsch-indische Kulturkontakte in Literatur, Religion und Politik, Berlin 1997

Prof. Dr. J. Peter Burgess has his origins in the USA and today lives in Norway. The literature scholar, social scientist and philosopher started his professional career in 1988. Since then he has worked at the International Peace Research Institute in Oslo (PRIO) and as an assistant professor at Volda University College in Norway. From 2003 to 2004 he was adjunct professor of cultural studies and philosophy at the University of Oslo, from 2006 to 2007 he held this position at the Fondation 'Nationale des Sciences Politiques' in Paris. Today Burgess is research pro-fessor of cultural studies and philosophy as well as leader of the Security Programme at PRIO, editor-in-chief of the magazine *Security Dialogue* by SAGE Pub-lications London and adjunct professor at the University of Trondheim/ Norway. In addition, he is a member of several institutions, societies and reference groups, for example of the Center for Peace and Human Security, the 'Institut d'études politiques' in Paris, of the project group for work against terrorism at the Norwegian Ministry of Foreign Affairs, of the European Union Studies Association, to name but a few. In his work, he deals with the European Union as a security community that seeks to save its values.

Publications i. a.:

The Ethical Subject of Security. Geopolitical Reason and the Threat to Europe, London 2010

Together with *Anthony Amicelle* et al: Promoting Human Security: Ethical, Normative and Educational Frameworks in Western Europe, Paris 2007

Culture and Rationality. European Frameworks of Norwegian Identity, Oslo 2001

(ed.): Cultural Politics and Political Culture in Postmodern Europe, Amsterdam 1997

Serap Çileli was born in Mersin/Turkey in 1966 and is now a German citizen. In 1968 her parents moved to Germany, while she and her siblings stayed in Turkey with their grandparents. At the age of 15 she was forced to an arranged marriage but found the possibility to get divorced in 1988. Afterwards, her mother took Çileli's two children to Germany. In 1991 she went to Germany herself, where at first she lived together with her parents and her children. But when her parents again wanted to force her to marry a man she did not know, she took her children and moved to a women's home. In 1993 she got married again, this time on her own choice. Since then she has stood up for the rights of women in Islam. She was one of the first women doing so and has a deep interest in sensitizing the public to this topic. In 2006 her book *Wir sind eure Töchter, nicht eure Ehre*, in which she describes her own experiences, was published in second edition. Çileli regards it as her duty to advise and support Turkish women, who are forced to marriage. For her dedication she received the Federal Cross of Merit in the year 2005 and as such is the youngest addressee of this award. In 2006 the regional capital Wiesbaden awarded her the Ludwig-Beck-Prize for Moral Courage and in doing so appreciated her struggle against honour killing. For her engagement for the security of Muslim women and therewith for the interior security of Germany she was honoured with the medal 'Bul le mérite' given to her by the Bund Deutscher Kriminalbeamter (BDK) in 2007.

Publications i. a.:

Eure Ehre – unser Leid. Ich kämpfe gegen Zwangsehe und Ehrenmord, München 2008

Wir sind eure Töchter, nicht eure Ehre, 4th edition, München 2006

Dr. Ralph Ghadban was born 1949 in Lebanon. After he had graduated in philosophy at the Lebanese University in Beirut in 1972 he came to Germany and is now a German citizen. He completed Islamic studies at the Freie Universität Berlin, where he received his Ph.D. in political sciences in the year 2000. Ghadban is one of the founders of the 'Libanonhilfe', an association that supports civil war refugees in Lebanon and Berlin. In his further professional career he amongst others was head of the advisory service for Arabs at the Diakonisches Werk Berlin, manager of the streetworking-project 'Gangway' as well as lecturer at the Berlin School of Economics and Law. Today the scholar of Islamic studies and journalist teaches at the Evangelische Fachhochschule Berlin and is a member of several committees, forums and teams. He for example belongs to the German Islam Conference (DIK) that serves as a platform for the dialogue between the German state and the immigrated Muslims. Migration research and integration are basic topics Ghadban deals with. He is focusing especially on minorities, Christians in the Muslim world and Muslims in the west. In the academic year 2008/2009 he was member of the Institute of Advanced Study in Princeton/USA where he conducted researches about the *fiqh* of Muslim minorities in the west.

Publications i. a.:

Den Islam neu denken, in: Das Parlament No. 32/33, Bonn August 2007

Tariq Ramadan und die Islamisierung Europas, Berlin 2006

Reaktionen auf muslimische Zuwanderung in Europa, in: Aus Politik und Zeitgeschichte, No. 26, Vol. 53, 2003, pp. 26-32

Die Libanon-Flüchtlinge in Berlin. Zur Integration ethnischer Minderheiten, Berlin 2000

Dr. Mario Gomez (LL.B.; LL.M.) is a member of the Law Commission of Sri Lanka. He was previously a lecturer in law at the University of Colombo where he taught administrative law, constitutional law, jurisprudence, and women's rights at undergraduate and post-graduate levels. He has published in the areas of public law, economic and social rights, women's rights, human rights commissions, internally displaced persons and public law. He has designed and conducted training programmes for judges, human rights activists, and staff of human rights commissions. He was a post-doctoral fellow at Harvard University in 2001/2002. He works as an independent human rights lawyer and is currently the lead researcher for a 'National Integrity study for Transparency International' and leading a study on land rights in eastern Sri Lanka.

Publications i. a.:

Together with *Rohan Edrisinha, V.T. Thamilmaran* and *Asanga Welikala* (eds.): Power Sharing in Sri Lanka: Constitutional and Political Documents 1926-2008 (Co-author). Berghof Foundation and Centre for Policy Alternatives, Berlin 2008, pp. 896

From Rhetoric to Realization, Delivering Socio-Economic Rights Through Courts and Commissions, in: *Raj Kumar/D.K. Srivastava* (eds.): Human Rights and Development, Law, Policy and Governance, Hong Kong 2006, pp. 65-94

National Human Rights Commissions and Internally Displaced Persons, illustrated by the Sri Lankan Experience, Brookings Institution, Washington D.C. 2002, pp. 36

Sri Lanka's New Human Rights Commission, in: Human Rights Quarterly, No. 2, Vol. 20, 1998, pp. 281-302

Dr. Necla Kelek was born in Istanbul/Turkey in 1957 and at the age of ten moved to Germany with her parents. After her apprenticeship as a design draftsperson she studied economics and sociology in Hamburg and Greifswald/Germany. In 2001 she did her Ph.D. about Islam in everyday life, whereupon she analysed the meaning of religion and tradition for Turkish youths living in Germany. In 2002 her dissertation was published. As a migration researcher and author, who fights for wom-en's rights, Kelek particularly is concerned with the topic integration and the aspect of parallel societies, and in doing so she cooperates with different institutions. She for example advises the legal authority of Hamburg when it comes to dealing with Turkish-Muslim prisoners. In addition, Kelek is a permanent member of the German Islam Conference. In 2005 her book *Die fremde Braut* was released, in which she writes about forced marriages and the judicial suppression of the woman in Islam in general. In the same year she received the Geschwister-Scholl-

Prize of Munich. In her work Kelek shows her critical opinion regarding the exercise of Islamic religion as well as the point of view and actions of some of her colleagues, which also was discussed through media. In a petition published in the weekly newspaper *Die Zeit* 60 migration researchers accused her of not arguing scientifically in her studies and publications and of generalising individual cases. Kelek reacted by writing an official letter: In her opinion, her adversaries follow an ideological concept of multiculturalism instead of turning against criminal activities such as forced marriages. Her book *Die verlorenen Söhne* was honoured with the international book-prize Corine in 2006. Furthermore, Kelek took over the Mercator-professorship at the University of Duisburg-Essen/Germany in 2006. Her latest book *Bittersüße Heimat* was published in 2008. In September 2009 she received the Hildegard-Von-Bingen-Prize of Mainz.

Publications i. a.:

Bittersüße Heimat. Bericht aus dem Inneren der Türkei, München 2009

Die fremde Braut. Ein Bericht aus dem Inneren des türkischen Lebens in Deutschland, 9th edition, Köln 2007

Die verlorenen Söhne. Plädoyer für die Befreiung des türkisch-muslimischen Mannes, 2nd edition, München 2007

Shigeko Kubota studied ethnology at Keio University in Tokyo/Japan between 1992 and 1997, and conducted fieldwork in India in 1996. In 1998 she started studying social anthropology and social sciences at Hitotsubashi University where she received her master's degree in 2000 and startet her Ph.D. at the Institute for the Study of Global Issues. In her work, Kubota observes how European and Asian cultures influence one another, and her special interest lies on the question, how Asian immigrants in Europe cope with the different cultural aspects. In 2003, she researched community changes in a foreign country within a Tibetan community in Switzerland and analyzed which way Europe is interested in Buddhism. Kubota is a member of The Japanese Society of Cultural Anthropology and of the Centre for New European Research, where she works as a fellow in the research group 'Europe outside Europe'. In this context she deals with the topic 'What is cultural collectivity? European Ideas of Tolerance and Intolerance', for which from 2005 to 2008 she received a scholarship by the Centre of Excellence Programme (COE).

Publications i. a.:

Non-Violence, Happiness and Health: The Contemporary Image of Tibet at Seen in 'The Dalai Lama in Hamburg 2007'; CNER Discussion Paper No. 43, February 2009

Religious Pluralism and the 'Religification' of Migrant Culture: Another Aspect of Multiculturalism in Europe; CNER Discussion Paper No. 30, September 2007

Buddhism in Europe; CNER Discussion Paper No. 24, March 2007

Somewhere Between Success and Neglect: The Social Existence of Tibet in Switzerland; CNER Discussion Paper No. 3, April 2005

Prof. Michael March was born in 1946 in New York, where he studied history at Columbia College, gaining his degree in 1968. Afterwards, he moved to Europe, living in London and writing for *The Guardian*, *Times Literary Supplement*, *The European* and *London Magazine*. In the late seventies, he created 'The Covent Garden Readings', bringing poets from central and eastern Europe to theatres in London. In 1989, March directed 'The Child of Europe Readings' at the National Theatre, which preceded the publication of two anthologies: *Child of Europe: A New Anthology of East European Poetry* and *Description of a Struggle: Contemporary East European Prose*. His work as a translator includes *Barbarian in the Garden* by Zbigniew Herbert and Gojko Djogo's *Ovid in Tomis,* which received a translation award from the National Endowment of the Arts. March currently lives in Prague where he directs the Prague Writers' Festival and is professor of poetry at New York University.

Publications i. a.:

The Way Back, Athens 2010

Only a Promise, Prague 2010

Disappearance, Athens 2003

Badr Mohammed was born in Beirut/Lebanon in 1966, came to Berlin together with his mother and his brothers and sisters in 1975 and is now a German citizen. He first completed an apprenticeship as a health inspector and emergency medical technician. Afterwards he studied interior design as well as health and social management. He completed postgraduate studies in intercultural management and is now social manager and secretary general of the European Integration Centre in Berlin-Brandenburg (EIZ). In 1991 Mohammed joined the Social Democratic Party (SPD) of Berlin. At state level he was member of the commission for immigration issues from 1992 to 1998 and afterwards founded the Corporation for Migration. In 2000 he built up the project group 'Arab Social Democrats Berlin' as well as the 'Initiative Group of new Germans', in 2003 he generated the 'Intercultural Forum of new Europeans'. Since 2006 Mohammed has been member of the chair of the German Islam Conference (DIK). In his opinion, German politics concerning integration should be reformed, as stated in the magazine *Welt Online* in June 2007. According to this, Mohammed expects from migrants who want to achieve German citizenship to learn the German language and to adhere to the law. But Mohammed also wants solutions for the European situation in general and sees the integration of immigrants and their families in the EU as an enrichment in cultural and economic terms, as he writes on the homepage of EIZ. In 2009, primarily for reasons of integration policy, he left the SPD and joined the CDU (Christian Democratic Union of Germany).

Prof. Dr. Susan Neiman was born in Atlanta, Georgia/USA. In 1982 she received her Master in philosophy at Harvard University and afterwards continued her graduate study at the Freie Universität Berlin. In 1986 she finished her Ph.D. in philosophy at Harvard University. She began her professional career in 1989 at Yale University, where she worked as assistant and as associate professor of philosophy until 1996. Afterwards, she was professor at Tel Aviv University from 1996 to 2000. Since then Neiman has been director of the Einstein Forum in Potsdam/Germany. Neiman is a member of the Berlin-Brandenburg Akademie der Wissenschaften, and serves on numerous advisory boards. Neiman's work is focused on moral and political philosophy as well as on the history of modern philosophy. Among her most important books are *Evil in Modern Thought,* translated into nine languages, and *Moral Clarity,* named by the *New York Times* as one of the most distinguished books of 2008. She has also published many articles and books on related topics, including *Fremde sehen anders. Zur Lage der Bundesrepublik.* In it she describes Germany's image abroad as more positive than many Germans realize. Her awards include the American Association of Publishers Scholarly and Professional Award for Philosophy in the year 2002 and the American Academy of Religion Award for Excellence in 2003, as well as a fellowship at the Institute of Advanced Studies in Princeton/New Jersey for 2006/2007.

Publications i. a.:

Moral Clarity. A Guide for Grownup Idealists, Harcourt 2008

Fremde sehen anders. Zur Lage der Bundesrepublik, Frankfurt am Main 2005

Evil in Modern Thought. An Alternative History of Philosophy, Princeton 2002

Sheela Patel was born in Mumbai (formerly Bombay)/India in 1952, where she still lives. She studied at the Tata Institute of Social Sciences in Mumbai and worked as a child counselor at the Nagpada Neighbourhood House, a community in the centre of Mumbai. In 1984 she founded the Society for the Promotion of Area Resource Centres (SPARC). She still is the President of this non-profit organization aiming at promoting equality and social justice for poor people in India, affording this part of the population education and participation in public life as citizens. In addition, Patel also started a project called SPARC Samudhaya Nirman Sahayak (SSNS) in 1999, that offers help with construction measures to slum dwellers in the cities. As part of her efforts to improve life in the slums she also turns her attention to Europe. An important part of her subject area is the development of so-called megacities, cities with more than 8 million inhabitants. Patel is member in the World Health Organization (WHO) since 2006, where she examines social prerequisites for health. In the same year she became head of a campaign of the Indian Ministry of Urban Development to improve the sanitary situation in urban areas. Patel is author of various articles where she mainly presents her work. Most recently she published together with Arif Hasan and others appropriate sanitation technologies for addressing deficiencies in provision in low- and middle-income nations (*Background Paper of the Human Development Report*, London).

Publications i. a.:

Squatting on the Global Highway: Community Exchanges for Urban Transformation, in: *Michael Edwards/John Gaventa* (eds.): Global Citizen Action, 2001, pp. 231-246

From Seed to Tree. Building Community Organisations in India's Cities, in: *Shirley Walters/Linzi Manicom* (eds.): Gender in Popular Education. Methods for Empowerment, London 1996, pp. 89-98

Prof. Dr. Minxin Pei studied at Shanghai International Studies University, at the University of Pittsburgh and at Harvard University, where 1991 he received his Ph.D. in political science. From 1992 to 1998 he taught politics at Princeton University. Today, Pei is director of the China Program at the Carnegie Endowment for International Peace in Washington D.C./USA. His areas of interest are especially the relations between the USA and China, the development of democratic political systems and Chinese politics. Furthermore, he is an expert concerning Asia, China and Taiwan, in security and foreign policy in China and its rule of law. He has published many articles for example in *Journal of Democracy*, *The National Interest* and *Foreign Affairs*. Pei is concerned with reforms and reformations in communist systems, and the ending of the Cold War.

Publications i. a.:

China's Trapped Transition. The Limits of Developmental Autocracy, Cambridge 2006

From Reform to Revolution. The Demise of Communism in China and the Soviet Union, Cambridge 1998

Bashy Quraishy was born in India, grew up in Pakistan and now lives in Copenhagen/Denmark. He studied engineering in Germany and the USA as well as international marketing in London and is now concerned with human rights, international understanding and the issues of ethnic minorities. He is chief editor of the magazine *MidiaWatch*, chairman of the media monitoring organisation and member of the Danish Human Rights Institute's Advisory Council. From 2001 to 2007 Quraishy was President of ENAR in Brussels, the European Network Against Racism. From 2005 to 2007, he sat on EU Commission's High Level Committee on the social and labour market integration of disadvantaged ethnic minorities in the EU. Besides, he is not only chairman of the 'European Platform for Jewish Muslim Cooperation', but also member of the board of trustees of the Dutch foundation 'More Colour in the Media' and board member of the international foundation 'Education for Life' in Israel. Regarding topics like ethnic minorities in the western world, multiculturalism, globalisation, etc., he publishes articles and offers a lot of contributions both in the Danish and in the European press. Furthermore, Quraishy is member of several commissions and working groups which deal with human rights, ethnic equality issues, integration's dilemma and anti-discriminating work in Denmark and other countries.

Publications i. a.:

Migration, Integration and the Role of Education, Bonn 2008

Dansk identitet. Set med brune øjne, Copenhagen 2003

Islam and Muslim Minorities in the Western Media. After the World Trade Center Attack, in: Nord-Süd aktuell, No. 4, Vol. 15, 2002, pp. 714-722

Prof. Dr. Caroline Y. Robertson-von Trotha was born in Glasgow/Scotland in 1951. She did an apprenticeship in hotel business and came to Germany at the age of 18. After her studies in sociology, political science, philosophy, and history in Heidelberg and Karlsruhe she completed her doctoral dissertation in sociology and habilitated at the University Karlsruhe (TH) in the year 2004. She was co-founder and between 1990 and 2002 managing director of the Interfacultative Institute for

Cultural Studies (IAK) at the University of Karlsruhe (TH). Since 2002 she has been founding director of the Centre for Cultural and General Studies (ZAK). Robertson-von Trotha amongst others is member of curatorship at the Institute for Cultural Politics of the Culture-Political Association and was associated member of the scientific advisory committee at the European Institute for Comparative Culture Research ERICarts. In addition, she is member of the governing board of the KIT Focus 'Humans and Technology' as well as spokeswoman of the KIT Competence Field 'Cultural Heritage and Dynamics of Change' within the Competence Area 'Technology, Culture and Society'. Since 2009 Robertson-von Trotha is vice-chairwoman of the Expert Committee Culture of the German Commission for UNESCO, member of the advisory board 'Diversity of Cultural Expression' and member of the EU Focus Working Group on Science and Culture. Her main topics of interest are multiculturalism, cultural change and globalisation, the mobilisation of ethnic identities and the transdisciplinary acquirement of competence. She is editor of the scientific series of the Centre for Cultural and General Studies *Kulturwissenschaft interdisziplinär/Interdisciplinary Studies on Culture and Society* and *Problemkreise der Angewandten Kulturwissenschaft.*

Publications i. a.:

Kulturerbe – Dilemmata des Bewahrens im Wandel, in: *Oliver Parodi/Gerhard Banse/Axel Schaffer* (eds.): Wechselspiele: Kultur und Nachhaltigkeit. Annäherungen an ein Spannungsfeld, Berlin 2010, pp. 263-274

Die Dialektik der Globalisierung. Kulturelle Nivellierung bei gleichzeitiger Verstärkung kultureller Differenz, Karlsruhe 2009

(ed.): Europa in der Welt – die Welt in Europa (= Kulturwissenschaft interdisziplinär/Interdisciplinary Studies on Culture and Society 1), Baden-Baden 2006

Prof. Dr. Mourad Wahba was born 1926 in Assiyut/Egypt. In 1948 he received his B.A. and in 1953 his Master's degree in philosophy at Cairo University. In 1956 he did his Ph.D. at Alexandria University. Wahba founded the Afro-Asian Philosophy Association (APA) in 1978, and is still its Honorary President today. Between 1993 and 2003 he was member of the Steering Committee of the International Federation of Philosophical Societies (FISP), in addition he serves as President to the Averroes and Enlightenment International Association, that he founded in 1994 together with Mona Abousenna. Today, he is Professor Emeritus of Philosophy at the Faculty of Education at Ain Shams University in Cairo/Egypt. Wahba edited several conference proceedings and is author of a number of books.

Publications i. a.:

Together with *Mona Abousenna* (eds.): Terrorism and Teaching Philosophy, Cairo 1999

Together with *Mona Abousenna* (eds.): Averoes and the Enlightenment, Amherst/ New York 1996

Zeitfracht Medien GmbH
Ferdinand-Jühlke-Straße 7
99095 Erfurt, Deutschland
produktsicherheit@kolibri360.de